Vertical Restraints in the Digital Economy

Vertical Restraints in the Digital Economy

Vertical Block Exemption Regulation Reform and the Future of Distribution

Edited by

Adina Claici
Denis Waelbroeck

Wolters Kluwer

Published by:
Kluwer Law International B.V.
PO Box 316
2400 AH Alphen aan den Rijn
The Netherlands
E-mail: international-sales@wolterskluwer.com
Website: lrus.wolterskluwer.com

Sold and distributed by:
Wolters Kluwer Legal & Regulatory U.S.
7201 McKinney Circle
Frederick, MD 21704
United States of America
Email: customer.service@wolterskluwer.com

ISBN 978-94-035-3243-1

e-Book: ISBN 978-94-035-3244-8
web-PDF: ISBN 978-94-035-3245-5

About the Global Competition Law Centre

College of Europe
Collège d'Europe

Brugge | Natolin

GCLC | Global Competition Law Centre

The Global Competition Law Centre (GCLC) forms part of the College of Europe and aims at promoting cutting-edge research in competition law and economics. It disseminates ideas and promotes research and benefits from a large network of competition professionals, built through the organisation of regular activities in Europe and elsewhere. Since its inception in January 2004, the GCLC has gained credentials as a high-level discussion forum for academics, practitioners, and enforcement officers in the competition field across the world. The GCLC regularly organises conferences, lunch talk seminars and evening policy talks, publishes books, and hosts a working papers series. In addition, the GCLC awards a yearly prize for the best dissertation in competition law and policy written at the College of Europe.

Editors

Adina Claici is a Visiting Professor at the College of Europe in Bruges and the Director of GCLC. She is an expert in competition economics and joined the competition service of Copenhagen Economics in 2017 as Managing Director of the Brussels office. Prior to that, Adina was a senior member of the chief economist team at DG Competition at the European Commission for nearly ten years. Adina is a regular speaker at conferences and has published numerous articles on various competition policy topics, in peer-reviewed academic journals and book chapters. She is also a Visiting Professor at Barcelona Graduate School of Economics. Adina has a PhD in Economics from Autonoma University of Barcelona.

Denis Waelbroeck is a Senior Partner in Ashurst LLP's EU and competition department in Brussels and has for forty years advised major clients in numerous sectors including healthcare, telecommunications, media, etc. He also has a major practice before the EU courts. In addition, he is a Professor of European Competition Law at the College of Europe in Bruges and at the Free University of Brussels. He has published several books and articles on EU law.

Contributors

Yves Botteman is a Belgian lawyer admitted in Brussels and New York. He focuses his practice on EU and national competition law, in particular, merger control and antitrust investigations as well as providing compliance advice, conducting audits and risk assessments. Specifically, Yves helps clients achieve their business objectives, by incorporating antitrust and competition law in their vision and strategy, corporate values and commercial practices. He provides strategic and practical advice to clients on new distribution models in the online space, where EU and national enforcement have been on the rise. He has significant experience counselling global and international trade associations, particularly on the design and implementation of industry-wide codes of conduct, standards and best practices. Over the years, he has gained substantial exposure to the media, entertainment, sports and leisure, smart mobility, and biotech industries.

Avantika Chowdhury is a Partner at Oxera Consulting based in London and Brussels. She has nearly fifteen years of experience in providing expert economic advice on competition matters and commercial disputes, including merger assessments, vertical and horizontal agreements and abuse of dominance cases in front of the European Commission and other competition authorities, and antitrust and damages litigation. Avantika has written widely on vertical restraints and led the research study on the topic published by the UK CMA. She has broad sectoral experience, with specific expertise in life sciences, technology, digital and intellectual property matters. Avantika has acted as expert in antitrust and damages litigation and in wider commercial disputes, including in front of the High Court in England, the UK Competition Appeal Tribunal, and courts in Ireland and the Netherlands. She holds an MSc in Quantitative Economics and a PhD in Economics, is listed in *The International Who's Who of Competition Lawyers & Economists* and is an active contributor to policy discussions through regular publications, speaking engagements and engagements in courses for judges and competition authorities.

Pablo Ibáñez Colomo is Professor of Law and Jean Monnet Chair in Competition and Regulation at the London School of Economics and Political Science. He is also a Visiting Professor of Law at the College of Europe (Bruges) and the Joint General Editor of the Journal of European Competition Law & Practice (Oxford University Press). He received a PhD from the European University Institute in June 2010 (Jacques Lassier Prize). Before joining the EUI as a Researcher in 2007, he taught for three years at the Law Department of the College of Europe (Bruges), where he also took an LLM in 2004. He has been a Visiting Professor at several institutions around the world, including Aix-Marseille University, Instituto Tecnológico Autónomo de México, Kobe University and Torcuato di Tella University.

Guillaume Duquesne is a Vice President at Compass Lexecon, based in Brussels. Since joining in 2013, He has advised clients on a wide variety of competition policy issues, covering sectors as diverse as energy, telecommunication, financial services, digital services, online platforms, and data services. He has advised clients in merger or antitrust cases at the European Commission level and at the level of the French competition authorities. Prior to joining Compass Lexecon, Guillaume worked as a quantitative analyst for Crédit Agricole – Corporate Investment Bank. He graduated the Ecole Normale Supérieure where he specialised in economics, mathematics and finance. He holds an MSc in Economics from the Paris School of Economics and an MSc in Quantitative Finance from Pierre and Marie Curie University.

Ian Forrester (General Court of the European Union 2015-2020) has been a practitioner, author, academic teacher and judge. He has lectured on EC/EU legal and policy topics in many countries and published extensively on these themes, particularly competition, customs, dumping, pharmaceuticals, sport, the precautionary principle and human rights. He has written over 100 articles and chapters which have been published in English, French, Japanese, Serbian and Spanish. He was appointed as an Honorary Professor and Honorary Doctor of Laws (2009) at Glasgow University, was appointed Queen's Counsel (1988) and Bencher, Middle Temple (2012). He has been the President of the Society of Franco British Lawyers since 2018. He was appointed by the UK, after a competitive process in 2020, to be included in the ICSID's Panel of Conciliators, available to help resolve international investment disputes. He has also served as an arbitrator in an ICSID matter.

In April 2015 he was nominated by the UK to be a member of the General Court of the Court of Justice of the European Union and was sworn in later that year. His mandate came to an end with Brexit in February 2020. While on the Court, he sat on about 230 cases touching trademarks, competition, terrorist asset freezes, agricultural subsidies, state aids, public procurement and civil service disputes. He was appointed a member of the newly created deontology committee of the Court and participated in drafting the Court's first Code of Conduct for judges, dealing with such matters as judicial conduct, possible conflicts and recusals, and the handling of hearings. He represented the Court on missions to other countries as well as participating in the collective activities of the Court serving twenty-eight countries with twenty-four official languages, employing 2,200 people.

When as a practising lawyer he participated in cases before courts or competition authorities or arbitral bodies in the UK, Belgium, Canada, France, Greece, Japan, Kosovo, Serbia and USA as well as the European institutions in Brussels and the three EU courts in Luxembourg. He was a member of the Bars of Scotland, New York, England and Brussels. He argued several leading cases in the fields of sport, computer software, pharmaceuticals, vehicles, public regulation, state aids, international trade, and publishing.

He was also involved in several European Court of Human Rights cases and he launched the pro bono practice of White & Case. He has been involved in at least thirty arbitration matters, either as advocate for a party, or as expert witness on European law, or as arbitrator, from 1983 to 2014.

Dr Miguel de la Mano is an Executive Vice President in Compass Lexecon's Brussels office. Before joining Compass Lexecon, Miguel was the Head of Economic Analysis and Evaluation at DG Internal Market. Since 2012, he has been leading a team of experienced financial economists in support of the EU Commission's unprecedented regulatory overhaul of EU banking, insurance, and financial markets. Miguel joined the European Commission in late 2000 as a competition economist. In 2003, he became a member of the newly created Chief Economist Team. He was appointed as Deputy Chief Economist in early 2009. From October 2011 to May 2012, he was the Acting Chief Economist at the UK Competition Commission.

Miguel has co-drafted guidelines setting out the European Commission's analytical framework on merger control, vertical and horizontal agreements (Article 101) as well as single firm conduct (Article 102). He also co-drafted 'guidelines on the submission on economic evidence' for DG COMP and the 'new market investigation guidelines for the former UK Competition Commission.

Over the last fifteen years, Miguel has been closely involved in dozens of in-depth merger and antitrust investigations, at the fact-finding, analysis, and decision making stages. He has defended the EU Commission in several court proceedings and provided economic testimony to EU Courts in several high profile antitrust and merger cases. He has written articles on EU competition policy and financial market regulation, with the aim of shaping and guiding EU enforcement and policymaking. While at Compass Lexecon, he has advised on many mergers, including Telia/Bonnier Broadcasting, E.On/Innogy, PostNL/Sandd, T-Mobile NL/Tele2 NL, Shire/Takeda, The Walt Disney Company/Twenty-First Century Fox, Deutsche Börse/LSE, Petrol/Geoplin, and NKT/ABB.

Miguel completed his graduate studies in economics at the Institute for World Economics in Kiel, Germany, and the European Institute at Saarbrucken University, Germany. He conducted his PhD research at Oxford University, UK.

Bernd Meyring is a Senior Competition Lawyer and the Managing Partner in Belgium at Linklaters LLP. He practices European and global competition law, with a particular focus on merger control and proceedings in the European Court of Justice, where he has represented clients in well over 100 cases in matters relating to competition law, financial regulation, environmental law and access to documents. He is a Professor of Competition Law at the College of Europe and the President of the College's Global Competition Law Centre.

Giorgio Monti is Professor of Competition Law at Tilburg Law School. He began his career in the UK (Leicester 1993-2001 and London School of Economics 2001-2010) before taking up the Chair in competition law at the European University Institute (EUI) in Florence, Italy (2010-2019). While at the EUI he helped establish the Florence Competition Program which carries out research and training for judges and executives. He also served as Head of the Law Department at the EUI. His principal field of research is competition law, a subject he enjoys tackling from an economic and a policy perspective. Together with Damian Chalmers and Gareth Davies he is a co-author of *European Union Law: Text and Materials* (4th ed., Cambridge University Press, 2019), one of the major texts on the subject. He is one of the editors of the *Common Market Law Review*.

Alexandra Prohm is a German lawyer. As a member of Dentons Europe LLP's Competition and Antitrust practice group, she works for the firm's Berlin and Brussels offices. She advises on all aspects of EU and German competition law and regularly assists clients in the energy and healthcare sectors. Alexandra focuses on merger control proceedings before both the European Commission and the German Federal Cartel Office and regularly coordinates multijurisdictional proceedings. Alexandra has also defended companies in antitrust and cartel proceedings before the European Commission and the EU courts. Prior to earning a master's degree in England and France, Alexandra studied French and German law. Since 2020, Alexandra teaches EU and German competition law at the University of Potsdam.

Prof. em. Dr Jacques Steenbergen (born in Antwerp (Belgium) in 1949) is the President of the Belgian Competition Authority since its establishment as an independent authority in 2013. From 2007 to 2013, he was the Director General of the Directorate General for Competition in the Belgian Ministry of Economic Affairs. He taught competition law at the University of Leuven from 1980 to 2014. Before joining the competition authority, he was a Partner in the Brussels office of Allen & Overy, and he has been legal secretary to the President of the Court of Justice under the presidency of Prof. J. Mertens de Wilmars.

He was also a member of the Bureau of the OECD Competition Committee from 2010 to 2020, is member of the board of editors and former editor-in-chief of the Dutch-Belgian European law review *SEW*, member of the scientific committee of the law review *Concurrences*, former chairman of the Board of the Stichting van het Koninklijk Conservatorium of Brussels (the foundation of the royal academy for music of Brussels), and honorary member of the Bar of Brussels (Nederlandse Orde van Advocaten bij de Balie te Brussel). He is a former member of the Brussels and Flemish Bar Councils.

He lectured or gave conferences and served as member of nomination or PhD examination committees in institutes and universities in Austria, Belgium, China, France, Hungary, Italy, the Netherlands, Poland, Romania, Slovenia, Spain, Switzerland, Turkey, the United Kingdom and the United States. He was also speaker or chairman at conferences in Australia, Brazil, Cyprus, the Czech Republic, Estonia, Germany, Greece, Japan, Latvia, Lithuania, Luxembourg, Malta, Morocco, Portugal, the Slovak Republic, Slovenia, Switzerland, and Tunisia. He publishes regularly on EU and competition law.

He obtained a PhD at the KU Leuven with Prof. Dr W. van Gerven on legal remedies and ailing industries (1978). He holds a Masters in Law from the KU Leuven (1972) and bachelor degrees or equivalent certificates in law, philosophy and economics from the University of Antwerp (UFSIA)(1969).

Summary of Contents

Table of Contents

Preface

This book appears concurrently with many responses to the Commission's consultation on potential policy choices that will underpin the reform of the Vertical Block Exemption.

Dual distribution, active sales restrictions, restrictions of online sales, price parity obligations, resale price maintenance, the duration of non-compete obligations and sustainability agreements are topics that have emerged as areas for conscious policy choices that may or may not diverge from the current rules. The GCLC's annual conference in January 2020 kick-started the debate on several of these topics and explored potential avenues for improvements.

Some of these topics have been discussed for as long as EU competition law has been enforced in the area of vertical restraints. For example, there has long been and there still is controversy around the strict approach to resale price maintenance, both at EU and at national level. The theories of benefit and harm are well established. The Commission has recognised potential areas of justification a decade ago. However, the examples have been lacking and it is therefore hard to evaluate the current approach. The online world may present some new challenges. Resale price maintenance is not a solution often discussed in this context. Rather, direct distribution and agency arrangements in online and off-line channels have become tools to avoid the EU's restrictive approach and lead to an allocation of resources that is driven by regulation more than by efficiency. But does this indicate that the established approach is too restrictive? Or rather that loopholes need to be closed? There is relatively limited change on this side of the debate and it seems uncertain whether the consultation can produce the game-changing evidence and examples that could underpin a shift in this well-established area.

There seems to be more tailwind for areas like dual distribution. The courts have become somewhat more open towards arrangements that incentivise brick and mortar distribution. Resale price maintenance has been discarded as a tool to secure margins. While some restrictions of online sales seem to have become tolerable in limited circumstances, this is currently not a game-changing solution and not on the cards at all in many industries. Applying different conditions to online and offline distributors is a course of action that many stakeholders seem to be willing to explore as it can sustainably preserve the availability of goods through both channels while at least partially addressing free-rider issues. It is also less restrictive than other measures that are being explored. We heard representatives from regulators advocating this route at the annual conference. The Commission is taking up the proposal and the next months will show how it can be framed more concretely.

The GCLC aims to put discussions on competition law and policy into a sound academic framework. It is in this spirit that our annual conference took stock of twenty years of modernisation of vertical restrictions and we heard about the role that courts have played in this context. We also explored similarities and differences between the objectives of competition and market integration, which have both played crucial roles in the development of the policy approach to vertical restraints. And we heard from enforcers on their long-term priorities and how the reform on vertical restraints can support them. We hope that the broader picture we have tried to set out can complement the various submissions and publications by stakeholders in the consultation process.

The GCLC is grateful for all the contributions that have made our 2020 annual conference a success. We also would like to thank our sponsors. Their contributions make our work possible.

Bernd Meyring
President GCLC

A Judicial Swan Song?

*Judge Ian Forrester**

Keynote speech delivered during the 15th GCLC Annual Conference on 30 January 2020, at Residence Palace in Brussels, Belgium.

This is a splendid event occurring at an acutely painful time. Splendid because the flower of the profession gathers to discuss the fascinating subject which has kept us nourished and stimulated and excited; splendid because of the august institution under whose auspices we meet. Painful because my country is on the verge of an uncertain political adventure which will reverberate for years to come. It is an honour to be here before such a gathering. Unlike Anthony speaking to the funeral crowd, I come not to bury or lament but to praise, to argue and to provoke. I am proud indeed to be the Judge from my country to serve on our Court, and proud to be the successor in office of Sir David Edward and Sir Nicholas

* These remarks at an academic gathering are purely personal and of course do not engage the place where I work. Thanks as ever are due to my colleagues in my cabinet, notably Cliona Hurley, generous and competent as ever, and also to Julian Ottekorts. For the avoidance of doubt, the examples I mention are totally hypothetical and imaginary.

Forwood; and correspondingly sad to be the last UK member of the Court, for the time being at least.

1 A LITTLE HISTORY

When I came to work at 23 Rue de la Loi, there were six Member States. Donald Holley, Richard Webster and Walter Oberreit were the patient teachers of young Euro-lawyers. German scholarship was quite dominant: Hartmut Johannes, Norbert Koch and Rudolf Graupner brought immense rigour to the new doctrines. Michel Waelbroeck was a celebrated teacher, author and practitioner. The first argument I attended was *Commercial Solvents*[1] (duty to supply a customer who had declined a proposal of commercial marriage) and the first cases which I submitted were *DCL/Bulloch*[2] (parallel trade and dual pricing in whisky), *Control Data*[3] (whether a computer could be a scientific instrument for purposes of avoiding customs duty in favour of research institutions) and *Bethel*[4] (the setting of air fares under International Air Transport Association (IATA) auspices). In my early appeals, I repeated the arguments made to the Commission with higher intensity. Subsequent cases were better remunerated (sometimes), better prepared (I hope), and equally exciting, though by no means regularly successful. In the whisky case, counsel were invited to join the Judges in the *salle de délibérés* for

1. Joined Cases 6 and 7/73, *Istituto Chemioterapico Italiano and Commercial Solvents v. Commission* (1974) ECR 00223.
2. Case 30/78, *Distillers Company Limited v. Commission* (1980) ECR 2229.
3. Case 294/81, *Control Data Belgium NV SA v. Commission* (1983) ECR 911.
4. Case 246/81, *Nicholas William, Lord Bethell, v. Commission* (1982) ECR 2277.

drinks after the argument. *Magill,*[5] *Bosman,*[6] *IMS,*[7] *Gibraltar,*[8] *GSK*[9] and *Microsoft*[10] were other thrills in the future. The hearings have also changed greatly: in the early days ninety minutes were granted, whereas today 10 or 15 minutes is the norm. In *Microsoft*, the entire week (24-28 April 2006) was devoted to the hearing. The focus of enforcement in Brussels and the nature of the controversies have changed greatly. The rules governing appeal much less so.

In the old days, high fines were deemed to show the toughness of the Commissioner. An annual tally of fines was proof of good enforcement. It was easier to settle cases after the Commissioner's fining target for the year had been reached, such that severity was no longer required in that calendar year.

Nowadays, fines are enormous by any measure. I feel that fines sometimes confuse the process by attributing guilt and stigma to what might be a choice of enforcement policy goals. They are, I suggest, far less important than media coverage suggests. Especially in Article 102 cases, the sting of the decision is the remedial conduct. It is the behavioural remedies which are likely to be far more important commercially and economically in terms of changing the business model

5. Joined Cases C-241/91 P and C-242/91 P, *Radio Telefis Eireann (RTE) and Independent Television Publications Ltd (ITP) v. Commission* (1995) ECR I-00743.

6. Case C-415/93, *Union royale belge des sociétés de football association ASBL v. Jean-Marc Bosman, Royal club liégeois SA v. Jean-Marc Bosman and others and Union des associations européennes de football (UEFA) v. Jean-Marc Bosman* (1995) ECR I-04921.

7. Case C-418/01, *IMS Health GmbH & Co. OHG v. NDC Health GmbH & Co. KG.* (2004) ECR I-05039.

8. Case C-298/89, *Government of Gibraltar v. Council* (1993) ECR I-03605.

9. Case C-53/03, *Synetairismos Farmakopoion Aitolias & Akarnanias (Syfait) and Others v. GlaxoSmithKline plc and GlaxoSmithKline AEVE* (2005) ECR I-04609.

10. Case T-201/04, *Microsoft Corp. v. Commission* (2007) ECR II-03601.

and achieving better conditions in the marketplace. Moreover, to the extent that the Commission is punishing wrongdoing as opposed to regulating a distorted marketplace, one might consider that the burden of proof should be higher. If that approach were correct, the infliction of a fine should increase the standard of excellence to be expected in the decision. Indeed, as I suggest below, where the decision is a policy choice in favour of one sector or a group of economic operators rather than another, the infliction of a fine inaccurately implies that the decision was easy or straightforward.

History, as well as common sense, favours the proposition that public authorities get it right most of the time. Before arriving in Luxembourg, I wrote critically about judicial deference to public authority in European Law. I do not want to resile from those concerns. *But* I have learned from being a member of the Court the difficulties faced by Judges in reconciling two approaches: a review of the legality of the acts of a very experienced and well-regarded administration, and the duty to examine the merits thoroughly.

2 LEGITIMACY

The rules are applied by a public authority, which is subject to judicial review by a court. The differences were and are important. The Commission is only an administration. It acts under the supervision of the Court. In the French administrative law tradition, judicial review of administrative action used to be relatively conservative and non-interventionist when compared to, for example, the common law tradition or the German tradition where authority flows from the rule's necessity and reasonableness. Judicial review is today evolving in several countries.

Whichever tradition we may favour, let me state as loudly as I can the following: the legitimacy of the enforcement activity of the institution depends on the existence of effective, genuine, visible judicial review. That is elementary, fundamental, crucial, and its importance is incapable of being exaggerated. Without the Court, the Commission's activity, no matter how skilled or well intentioned, risks being called arbitrary, illegitimate, unjust.

In a democracy, the public authority must sometimes lose in its own courts. We do not respect electoral or judicial systems which record success for the government 99% of the time. I absolutely reject the notion that finding against the Commission lowers public respect for the institution. To the contrary, the public is likely to be comforted by the fact that the institutional system involves robust quality control. It is unfortunate that the Commission's record in Article 102 cases was 100% for some thirty years. Of course, a prosecutor will win the majority, likely a large majority, of its cases. But it is absolutely not the case that rigorous quality control reduces confidence in the service. This is all the more certain where 'competition law' is rooted in a constitutional text, the few lines of Articles 101 and 102, which have been interpreted differently around the world over the years. Past decisions, past judgments and academic writings offer a framework for analysing how to examine a controversy. Competition law is not tax law, nor is it chemistry, and it is certainly not mathematics. It is an approach to solving a dispute where parties are said to be acting in a manner which may damage the public interest. We should not believe that judicial setbacks weaken the authority: to the contrary, reversals confirm legitimacy.

In our world, the European Commission intervenes after balancing noisy, articulate, well-funded and very varied interest groups. The Commission will almost never have no legal basis for its action. There will almost always be a pile of letters, studies and charts on each side of the argument. So there are situations where the choice between the factions is a choice of conflicting or alternative public policies. Shall the institution favour intellectual property or consumer choice? Pharma innovators (good for new medicines) or pharma generics (good for budget)? Shall the relevant market include both hybrid cars and electric cars, or only one? That last choice may determine whether Article 102 is applicable and as a result whether abuse occurred.

A big competition case will often be delicately balanced inside the institution. There will be critics (and supporters) in the house, in the Legal Service, in different Commissioners' offices, lobbying by Members of the European Parliament (MEPs), Member States, the press, NGO groups and trade associations. There will be those who favour investment in the sector or feel the complainant will not look good or feel there is going to be Member State reluctance to see the condemnation of another big producer in that field or that part of the world. The law will be helpful, but never perfectly relevant. The facts will never be unequivocal. But the authority has to decide. If it is going one way, it will produce a condemnation which presents the case as darkly as is consistent with its own procedural rules. There is maybe a tendency to be as negative as possible, making as many accusations as possible, to paint a moral case. Although the concept of abuse is said to be an objective one, I have always taught students that an element of wrongdoing is an element in every Article 102 case.

Fashions change, not just enforcement priorities, but substantive legal questions also: think of compulsory licensing, which totally changed from *Volvo/Veng*[11] to *Magill*[12] to *IMS*[13] to *Microsoft.*[14] Think of the evolution of rules on rebates, from *Roche Vitamins*[15] via *British Airways*[16] to *Intel.*[17] Think of the modalities of enforcement: no more notifications, no provisional validity, no comfort letters. Think of the expanded role of the Hearing Officer: access to the file, confidentiality, timing and notice. The law and its application in a specific case are not timeless or unchanging. The words of Articles 101 and 102 are interpreted to mean different things. The Court's job is to oversee whether the new interpretation is valid.

We can also note that there are plenty of sources of new decisions and new interpretations of the duties of dominant players from other jurisdictions. EU national courts and authorities co-apply the EU competition rules. The Treaty of Rome's Articles 85 and 86 (now 101 and 102) have been replicated with some tweaks in the national competition laws of many third countries, I think more than 100. American, Australian, Korean and South African courts and agencies will apply parallel concepts, with different concerns or different outcomes (or similar ones). Thus there is every reason to be open to the proposition that the European Commission got it

11. Case 238/87, *AB Volvo v. Erik Veng (UK) Ltd.* (1988) ECR 6211.
12. Joined Cases C-241/91 P and C-242/91 P, *Radio Telefis Eireann (RTE) and Independent Television Publications Ltd (ITP) v. Commission* (1995) ECR I-00743.
13. Case C-418/01, *IMS Health GmbH & Co. OHG v. NDC Health GmbH & Co. KG.* (2004) ECR I-05039.
14. Case T-201/04, *Microsoft Corp. v. Commission* (2007) ECR II-03601.
15. Case 85/76, *Hoffmann-La Roche & Co. AG v. Commission* (1979) ECR 0461.
16. Case C-95/04 P, *British Airways plc v. Commission* (2007) ECR I-02331.
17. Case T-286/09, *RENV, Intel Corporation v. Commission* (case in progress).

wrong in a specific case and even more open to the concept that reasonable persons may reasonably differ as to the wisdom, rightness or solidity of a particular controversial decision.

The rulings of the Court of Justice on competition cases are frequently more liberal than rulings on appeals to our Court. This may seem surprising. It illustrates the fact that there is a difference between considering whether a particular enforcement decision was justified in the one case and in the other case giving abstract guidance in principle to a national court asking whether, for example, it is anticompetitive to lease a shop on condition that no other supermarket can rent space in that shopping mall.

The Commission is very conscious of judicial review. Every setback in Luxembourg is taken very seriously. So both the Commission and the Tribunal operate in the shadow of judicial review. Our Court has been criticised for being insufficiently rigorous in how it has handled some appeals. And that leads us to the problem of deference.

If we go back 2,500 years, we can find in Greek tragedy the words 'Let no man live uncurbed by law or curbed by tyranny'. If we go back seventy-seven years, we can read a famous dissent by a famous judge in a famous case. Mr Liversidge[18] was arrested during wartime, on 29 May 1940, on the grounds that the Secretary of State had reasonable cause to believe that he was of 'hostile origin or association'. The Minister declined to describe his grounds for ordering the arrest. It sufficed that he said he had reasonable cause. Mr Liversidge, a volunteer RAF officer who had Russian relatives (he had changed his name from Persweig) and had had some

18. *Liversidge v. Anderson* (1942) AC 206.

German business connections (and was maybe thought to be a bit louche), brought an action for false imprisonment after he had been released from custody. Probably there was some embarrassment on the official side: someone had blundered or been over-zealous. He lost at first instance and appealed unsuccessfully up the English court hierarchy to the House of Lords. The times were dramatic. The House of Lords had been bombed and the Law Lords met in emergency accommodation. Was the Minister obliged to explain how or why? He said he had 'reasonable cause to believe'. Was his mere assertion of being satisfied enough? Four Law Lords supported the Minister: times were grave, there was an emergency, this was no time to relax vigilance, and the Minister had in good faith exercised a not unlawful discretion. *Arma clamant, leges tacent* was the Government's posture: in time of war we cannot be too fussy about due process. Plenty of Supreme Court judges would have been tempted to do the same (*see Korematsu v. United States*[19]). But Lord Atkin dissented in terms which caused a stir:

---

19. *Fred Korematsu v. United States*, 320 U.S. 81, 91-932 (1943). In the aftermath of Pearl Harbor, military areas were created to exclude all persons of Japanese ancestry on the basis of an Executive Order. The petitioner, an American citizen of Japanese descent, was convicted in a federal district court for remaining in one of these newly created 'military areas'. The exclusion order was confirmed as constitutional by the Court in the light of war and national security. Effectively imprisoning citizens by reference to their ethnic or racial status was obviously horribly sensitive. Justice Robert Jackson dissented:

> A military order, however unconstitutional, is not apt to last longer than the military emergency. Even during that period a succeeding commander may revoke it all. But once a judicial opinion rationalizes such an order to show that it conforms to the Constitution, or rather rationalizes the Constitution to show that the Constitution sanctions such an order, the Court for all time has validated the principle of racial discrimination in criminal procedure and of transplanting American citizens. The principle then lies about like a loaded weapon ready for the hand of any authority that can bring forward a plausible claim of an urgent need.

> 'Reasonable cause' for an action or a belief is just as much a positive fact capable of determination by a third party as is a broken ankle or a legal right. ... In this country, amid the clash of arms, the laws are not silent. They may be changed, but they speak the same language in war as in peace. It has always been one of the pillars of freedom ... that the judges are no respecters of persons and stand between the subject and any attempted encroachments on his liberty by the executive, alert to see that any coercive action is justified in law.

The speech of Lord Atkin, as we now see it, was evidently on the right side of the slope of history. Now, decisions in the context of wartime emergencies cannot be compared to determining whether in peace time a company must pay a fine, divest a business or deal against its will. But it remains a vivid example of the timelessness of the proposition that judges are meant to disagree with the public authority for the benefit of all. I very strongly disagree with the notion that criticising government action judicially is unpatriotic or subversive or disrespectful.

3 THE DEFERENCE BUSH

One topic perpetually debated among EU lawyers has been the extent to which the public authority enjoys the right to exercise its discretion and to what extent those choices are susceptible of judicial review. In the seminal case of *Grundig Consten*,[20] the Court said (more or less) that the Commission was entitled to make a policy priority of enhancing parallel trade by treating obstacles thereto as infractions. Variants of

---

Every repetition imbeds that principle more deeply in our law and thinking and expands it to new purposes.

20. Joined Cases 56 and 58-64, *Établissements Consten S.à.R.L. and Grundig-Verkaufs-GmbH v. Commission* (1966) ESE 299.

this doctrine have been voiced in many cases. In *Remia*,[21] the Court repeated this doctrine in endorsing the reasonableness of the Commission's determination of the proper duration of a non-compete clause. This tolerant examination of administrative action, the according of a generous margin of discretion, was often called 'light judicial review'. In subsequent cases, the deference doctrine multiplied like a luxuriant plant. The plant became an overgrown bush in *Microsoft*[22] in which the formulation of light judicial review was extended to technical matters, not merely complex economic assessments. There were in that case hotly debated factual matters concerning the design of computer operating systems, how software functions, the role of directories in networks of servers, why media functionality was or was not included in an operating system, and other topics. While these matters were assuredly technical and complex, they were well understood. The issues at stake were set forth with limpid clarity in the admirably accurate Report for the Hearing. The judges of the Court of First Instance were evidently able to decide on the merits of the case, as they had accurately identified the issues in dispute. But the Court announced an abstentionist approach:[23]

> The Court observes that it follows from consistent case-law that, although as a general rule the Community Courts undertake a comprehensive review of the question as to whether or not the conditions for the application of the competition rules are met, *their review of complex economic appraisals made by the Commission is necessarily limited to checking whether the relevant rules on procedure and on stating reasons have been complied with, whether the facts have been*

21. Case 42/84, *Remia BV and others v. Commission* (1985) ECR 2545.
22. Case T-201/04, *Microsoft Corp. v. Commission* (2007) ECR II-03601.
23. *Ibid*, §87-89.

> *accurately stated and whether there has been any manifest error of assessment or a misuse of powers …*
>
> *Likewise, in so far as the Commission's decision is the result of complex technical appraisals, those appraisals are in principle subject to only limited review by the Court, which means that the Community Courts cannot substitute their own assessment of matters of fact for the Commission's* (see, as regards a decision adopted following complex appraisals in the medico-pharmacological sphere, order of the President of the Court of Justice in Case C-459/00 P(R) Commission v Trenker (2001) ECR I-2823, paragraphs 82 and 83).
>
> However, while the Community Courts recognise that the Commission has a margin of appreciation in economic or technical matters, that does not mean that they must decline to review the Commission's interpretation of economic or technical data. The Community Courts must not only establish whether the evidence put forward is factually accurate, reliable and consistent but must also determine whether that evidence contains all the relevant data that must be taken into consideration in appraising a complex situation and whether it is capable of substantiating the conclusions drawn from it (see, to that effect, concerning merger control, Case C-12/03 P Commission v Tetra Laval [2005] ECR I-987, paragraph 39).

So, back in 2007, these paragraphs expanded the Courts' deference to include complex *technical* appraisals as well as complex economic ones. The familiar standard was set forth accurately in §87 referring to 'complex economic appraisals' where the review is 'necessarily limited to checking whether the relevant rules … have been complied with, whether the facts have been accurately stated and whether there has been a manifest error of appraisal'.

I suggest we should distinguish between, on the one hand, intensity of control which inevitably involves a respect for the discretion naturally accorded to a specialised public authority and, on the other hand, the invocation of complexity as a reason for abstaining from doing our duty. Thus, where the Commission after looking at the impact of a non-compete clause decides that twenty-four months is more appropriate than eighteen months or thirty months, it would be a bold judge who set aside that determination. By contrast, electing to refrain from looking closely at technical arguments on the basis that the authority probably was correct in that the topic is complex would be very unfortunate.

Saying in effect that 'since this is very technical we are going to stay away from looking at it closely' maybe was included as a convenient additional reason to reject an appeal. The sentence about light judicial review has sometimes appeared where in actual practice the Court had indeed considered the merits with care (as was the case in *Halcor/Chalkor*[24]). I suggest that the phrase may actually weaken the credibility of the judgment, rather than strengthening it. And I am sure that the *justiciable*'s confidence in the judicial process will be diminished by its presence.

4 COMPETITION AND CASELOADS

My Court was established to respond to criticism that the Court of Justice was not giving enough time to the fact-rich big dossiers that were coming up from the Commission, notably in competition and anti-dumping cases in the 1980s. As things turned out, dumping cases have been only 1.63 % of our workload in the last five years.[25] Competition cases were

24. Case C-386/10 P, *Chalkor AE Epexergasias Metallon v. Commission*, OJ C 32, 4.2.2012, pp. 9–9.

25. Seventy-three out of 4,468 cases lodged in 2014-2018 before the General Court, *see* European Commission, *Annual Reports from the Commission to the Council and the European Parliament on the EU's Anti-Dumping, Anti-Subsidy and Safeguard activities 2014-2018*, https://eur-lex.europa.eu/ (last accessed 23 January 2020); Court of Justice, *Annual Report 2018 Juridical Activity*, p. 235, https://curia.europa.eu/jcms/upload/docs/application/pdf/2019-04/_ra_2018_en.pdf (last accessed 23 January 2020).

until recently quite few in number.[26] Things have changed, however. We currently have *Intel,*[27] *Lithuanian Railways,*[28] three *Google* cases,[29] two *Qualcomm* cases,[30] *Bulgarian gas pipelines,*[31] and several challenges to the rejection of a complaint (*Fakro/Velux,*[32] *Carpenter/Subaru,*[33] *Sped-Pro/PKP Cargo*[34] and *DesignLed/Philips*[35]).

These are very large matters, and they reflect the fact that today the European Commission has a good claim to be the most innovative/radical/dynamic antitrust agency in the world. Its decisions in *Volvo/Veng,*[36] *Magill,*[37] *Tetrapak,*[38] *Microsoft*[39] and *British Airways*[40] have set new standards. Brussels is unquestionably one of the world's top cities for creativity in the enforcement of the competition rules.

---

26. The number of competition cases was 17 in 2015, 18 in 2016, 38 in 2017 and 28 in 2018, Court of Justice, *Annual Report 2018 Juridical Activity*, p. 236 https://curia.europa.eu/jcms/upload/docs/application/pdf/2019-04/_ra_2018_en.pdf (last accessed 27 January 2020).
27. Case T-286/09, RENV, *Intel Corporation v. Commission.*
28. Case T-814/17, *Lietuvos geležinkeliai v. Commission.*
29. Cases T-612/17, T-604/18 and T-334/19, *Google and Alphabet v. Commission.*
30. Cases T-235/18 and TT-671/19, *Qualcomm v. Commission.*
31. Case T-136/19, *Bulgarian Energy Holding and Others v. Commission.*
32. Case T-515/18, *Fakro v. Commission.*
33. Case T-531/18, *LL-Carpenter v. Commission.*
34. Case T-791/19, *Sped-Pro v. Commission.*
35. Case T-886/19, *Design Light & Led Made in Europe and Design Luce & Led Made in Italy v. Commission.*
36. *Supra* n. 11.
37. Joined Cases C-241/91 P and C-242/91 P, *Radio Telefis Eireann (RTE) and Independent Television Publications Ltd (ITP) v. Commission* (1995) ECR I-00743.
38. Case T-83/91, *Tetra Pak International SA v. Commission* (1994) ECR II-00755.
39. Case T-201/04, *Microsoft Corp. v. Commission* (2007) ECR II-03601.
40. Case C-95/04 P, *British Airways plc v. Commission* (2007) ECR I-02331.

Yet at the same time, I believe that the Commission is a procedurally cautious body, despite the boldness of some of the positions it takes. It is not reckless, even though it may be controversial. It is easier, so I have heard, to stop something inside DG Comp than to start something novel. The Legal Service has an important voice, internal consultations can be prolonged, Devil's Advocate panels may be needed, other services may have their word to say, NGOs, competitors and allies will submit extensive arguments. So the head of the case team has to work hard to pilot the decision along the tortuous road to adoption and press release. However, those internal checks and balances, which are genuine and demanding, are procedurally invisible to the *justiciable*. So we have an intellectually creative and well-respected agency, which strongly wishes to avoid judicial criticism, in charge of enforcing competition rules in important new cases. It is pointless to pretend that the Commission's Directorate General for competition is some kind of wild beast which preys on American interests. That said, the procedure by which decisions are taken is unique in the world of competition law.

Before considering in detail how the Commission's decision-making in competition cases is structured, I will make two overarching comments. First, the quality of judicial review of administrative action should be judged by reference to the entirety of the process from first complaint to final appeal. The weaker the administrative part, the stronger is the need of rigorous review on appeal, and vice versa: that is effectively a question of legitimacy. Second, we might usefully speculate on whether in a remote future a board of appeal or other extra step in competition decision-making in Brussels could improve the situation in Luxembourg.

5 HOW DECISIONS IN COMPETITIONS CASES ARE TAKEN BY THE EUROPEAN COMMISSION

So let us recall where things stand today. In my early days in Brussels, a common criticism was that the Commission was 'prosecutor, judge and jury': this assumed that the process before the Commission was a trial in which case the 'prosecution' and the 'trial' and the 'sentence' were handled by the same people. Such arguments, as we now see them, confused the administrative phase and the judicial phase of the case. The more accurate question would have been whether the administrative procedures' alleged imperfections were rendered irrelevant by the availability of close judicial oversight.

One feature to note is the hearing. It is presided by the Hearing Officer, usually a very experienced and well-regarded official. However, the hearing is functionally not a trial in which a trier of fact decides between two conflicting assertions. It is an opportunity for an accused company to suggest to the case team that after all they were mistaken, and that their three years of effort in bringing the case thus far had been in vain as the case was dropped. Thus, the Hearing Officer is there to ensure fair play at the hearing but not to decide whether Mr Dupont was at the suspicious meeting in the Hilton on 13 January.

Second, the decision is made by the Commission as a college, so a finding of guilt is made by a group of twenty-eight eminent political figures, of whom one is fully informed about the case. This is more of a curiosity than a glaring vice.

And a third frequently noted problem is the composition of the case team, where the same officials may be responsible for handling the first complaint, investigating, gathering documents, framing the charges and organizing the final decision imposing a condemnation and a fine. I note that these features have been repeatedly endorsed judicially in Luxembourg. However, in France, the attribution of multiple inconsistent responsibilities in competition enforcement has been criticised. We can note a decision of the French *Conseil Constitutionnel* on whether the national telecoms regulator could impose penalties. The *Conseil* ruled that the lack of separation of powers in investigating (*les fonctions de poursuite et d'instruction*) and punishing (*les fonctions de jugement*) exercised by the regulator would breach the principle of impartiality guaranteed by Article 16 of the *Déclaration des Droits de l'Homme et du Citoyen de 1789*. Thus, it is by no means obvious that as a matter of due process, the mechanisms by which fines are imposed are satisfactory.[41] It is also obvious that regardless of whether we would start today with a different structure, there is no prospect of dramatic change. My personal view is that the hearing could significantly be adapted to acknowledge the sentiments of enterprises and their lawyers who aspire to a more *contradictoire* structure.

---

41. Conseil Constitutionnel, Décision No. 2013-331 QPC du 05 juillet 2013, *Société Numéricâble SAS et autre*, §12:

> Considérant que, selon le premier alinéa de l'article L. 132 du code des postes et des communications électroniques, les services de l'Autorité de régulation des communications électroniques et des postes sont placés sous l'autorité du président de l'Autorité; que, selon l'article D. 292 du même code, le directeur général est nommé par le président de l'Autorité, est placé sous son autorité et assiste aux délibérations de l'Autorité; que, par suite et alors même que la décision de mise en demeure relève du directeur général, les dispositions des douze premiers alinéas de l'article L. 36-11 du code des postes et des communications électroniques, qui n'assurent pas la séparation au sein de l'Autorité entre, d'une part, les fonctions de poursuite et d'instruction des éventuels manquements et, d'autre part, les fonctions de jugement des mêmes manquements, méconnaissent le principe d'impartialité; que celles de ces dispositions qui sont de nature législative doivent être déclarées contraires à la Constitution.

The European Convention on Human Rights (ECHR) permits administrative measures which impose penalties at first instance, provided that on appeal there remains available judicial review by independent judges. The *Menarini*[42] judgment of the ECHR states that penalties in competition cases can be imposed, provided that there is available on appeal a control of fact in law, in principle complete. (There may be a question as to whether truly penal matters can be decided administratively.)

Now, our Court's structure, its Treaty-ascribed competence and our working practices provide in essence for a review of legality. Article 263 of the Treaty on the Functioning of the European Union (TFEU) gives competence 'on grounds of lack of competence, infringement of an essential procedural requirement, infringement of the Treaties or of any rule of law relating to their application, or misuse of powers'. Article 261 gives us *pleine juridiction* (unlimited) where sanctions are applied.

6 THE TRIBUNAL'S ROLE

Assume there is an appeal. We look at the *moyens* (pleas in law) and their several *branches*. We answer each of the *moyens* and address each *branche*. We may or may not frontally address the core question of fact or law which is presented. If the lawyers have done a poor job, they may have not well framed a procedurally valid analysis of the rightness or not of the decision's various elements. One question which we confront regularly is what to do if the application has not made the best of the available legal arguments.

42. *A. Menarini Diagnostics S.r.l. v. Italy* – 43509/08, ECHR 2011-II.

The Court has frequently noted, when upholding a decision, the absence of illegality, the absence of manifest error and the formal respect for applicable procedural rules. As I note above, such a conclusion is, as a matter of technical administrative law formalism, valid. But it may not respond to the requirement of a check 'in principle complete' as to the merits in fact and law. These cases may be of enormous economic or social significance. So we may have a decision which imposes major burdens on the undertaking or refuses to intervene and thereby aggrieves the complainants. Let us assume that time limits, confidentiality and access to the file are all clear. The issue of whether the Commission reached what we might call a sound decision remains.

Can our Courts elect to overturn a policy choice on the grounds that although the authority acted conscientiously it reached the wrong conclusion, erred, was too severe or too mild, failed to consider the right principles? Can we substitute a different finding than the one made by the Commission?

There is a delicate balance. If we do no more than check the legality of the decision, then we may in effect be renouncing our duty to effect a control of fact and law in principle complete. But if we decide – for example – that hybrid and electric cars were wrongly attributed to the same relevant market, we are overruling an expert agency which has carefully considered and has reached the opposite conclusion.

A related and more acute question concerns infringements *by object*, being those infringements which are so obviously inexcusable that there is no need to examine their alleged pro-competitive effects or justifications. I suggest that if indeed there is a problem of legitimacy as to administrative condemnations, this is even graver where the finding is of a *by object* infringement, a breach of the law so obvious and so inexcusable that no proffered justification need be taken seriously. A first instance finding that endorses as within the administration's margin of discretion, without close enquiry, an inexcusable economic crime, troubles me.

7 OTHER APPELLATE COMPETENCES

There are over thirty agencies established across the EU dealing with the process of reaching consistency between twenty-eight national approaches to common problems, such as food safety (Parma), medicines (London, now Amsterdam), trademarks (Alicante), plant varieties (Anger). Some of them are highly technical and economically significant (medicines, dangerous chemicals, feed additives). Some of these agencies offer a degree of internal review, which can greatly facilitate subsequent judicial review. When our Court receives a trademark appeal from European Union Intellectual Property Office (EUIPO) in Alicante, we are a third instance body checking a file of maybe fifty pages and ten annexes. A competition appeal may well involve 1,000 pages of pleadings plus annexes, charts, expert reports, and, much more importantly, a mixing up in the decision of the trivial and anecdotal with the crucial. Yet we are doing the appeal at first instance. I invite reflection about the possibility of instituting some internal *contradictoire* process in Brussels; this may be a good idea or a bad idea, but I suggest that we ought never to exclude consideration of reforms.

8 WINNER TAKES ALL? OR YES, BUT ON THE OTHER HAND?

There may be several policy choices in the administrative decision. It might be bad news for cross-border trade in books or good news for investment or green recycling or access to technical information by independent repair shops or sellers of luxury perfumes or online shopping apps.

The institution will have balanced these points in writing its decision. A wise authority notes both sides of an argument. Our judgments, by contrast, often read in what I call a 'Winner takes all' manner: the applicant is wrong and its complaints are groundless. The reader may think that it was a waste of time even to have come to court. But in truth the Chamber was perhaps doubtful and may have had difficulty in reaching consensus. If the Commission has appeared casual about the interests of railway passengers or copyright collection societies or sports federations or online shopping apps or has favoured their rivals' approach, this Court should properly be wondering whether the Commission went too far or not far enough. Our judgment ought to reflect that awareness that balances have to be struck: on the one hand, on the other hand. I suggest that it is better for us to echo the questions in that debate than to pretend we lack the authority to do so and thus hide behind the theory that we are not equipped legally or materially to assess such matters. Moreover, when reaching a conclusion has been difficult, we do ourselves no service by pretending the outcome was obvious. Noting the presence of valid competing arguments enhances the conviction of the ultimate decision.

Big competition cases rarely present binary problems and are never going to be easy. I suggest that our judgments may have the tendency to underestimate the arguments of the party whose cause is not going to prevail. The totality of its *moyens* need not necessarily be the totality of the merits of its case. I am fond of citing Vice Chancellor Megarry, a wise and generous judge who loved literature. He used to ask visitors to identify the most important person in his court, the answer being the person who is going to lose. We should write to explain to that person or entity what and why we have decided.

9 LIGHT JUDICIAL REVIEW: THE UNPRUNED BUSH

Saying we cannot go behind the policy decision in this case is much less persuasive and satisfactory than saying 'While it is correct as the applicant states that this measure may have the effect of making it more difficult for sports clubs to raise sponsorship, the Commission has pointed out that the applicant itself has succeeded in obtaining sponsorship despite the burdens established.' I suggest that it is inappropriate for us to present the outcome as obvious. That was a formalist vice of administrative law. We have maybe slipped into it by merely observing that the authority had the legal power to act in a certain way and that what it did was not unlawful. This debate is not new and not peculiar to Luxembourg. In the 1960s and 1970s, French administrative law was extremely conservative. For example, if a novel argument appeared during the subsequent litigation, the court might well decline to consider it. Other procedural obstacles, what we might call formalist, were strictly applied. That has radically changed in France. Now, sometimes, our Court declines to consider arguments made tardily or only implicitly made. *Ne ultra petita* is a doctrine which we sometimes apply quite severely.

Being strict on novel arguments or strict on admissibility matters may have the effect of denying the adumbration of important judicially ready controversies. They may, of course, also have the effect of not wasting time on hopeless theories.

Popular expectations of courts are evolving. The UK Supreme Court has unanimously annulled the advice of the Prime Minister to the Crown on whether to suspend Parliament. That step surprised my colleagues in some Member States. Others were enthusiastic. If we are not to have dissenting judgments, at least let us admit that reaching a conclusion was not without difficulty. That is guidance and perhaps a warning for the future. Yes, in this case we did agree that it was crucial to help hotel owners promote their own sites, but we recognise the merits of platforms like the intervenor's and in a future case we do not exclude that the concerns of platform operators might require more flexibility and so on. These words of caution can help the law evolve in a gradual, non-jerky, manner.

10 AN EXAMPLE FROM ANTI-DUMPING

The criteria for comparing Normal Value and Export Price, the two critical parameters in determining if dumping has occurred, are deeply controversial. They are said by their detractors to have the effect of creating a dumping margin and not of revealing a dumping margin. The comparison is meant to achieve a fair comparison. If the criteria have the effect that selling at the same price on both the home and the export market (after making parallel deductions on both sides) then it is clear that the fairness of the exercise is debatable. It can be justified, but it is controversial. But in *IKEA Wholesale*[43] we read:

> The choice between the different methods of calculating the dumping margin, or the determination of the existence of harm require an appraisal of complex economic situations and the judicial review of such an appraisal must therefore be limited to verifying whether relevant procedural rules have been complied with, whether the facts on which the contested choice is based have been accurately stated, and whether there has been a manifest error in the appraisal of those facts or a misuse of powers.

In the realm of measures to protect trade, the Community institutions enjoy a broad discretion by reason of the complexity of the economic, political and legal situations which they have to examine (*see*, to that effect, *Fediol v. Commission*[44] and *Nachi Fujikoshi v. Council*[45]).

For the Court to say that these calculations are too complex to be reviewed is a surrender of the duty of the Court to review rigorously executive action. Of course, there is a broad discretion. Of course, we must assume good faith on the part of the investigators and their masters. But that does not mean that we can say 'it is all very difficult and therefore we cannot examine whether the basis for making the comparison between Normal Value and Export Price was fair'. If the Council decides it is politically opportune to go ahead or not to go ahead, then the Court will likely accede in most cases to that choice. But we should not say that we cannot understand and therefore need not or cannot examine whether three Normal Value sales at 7, at 8, and at 9 dollars

43. Case C-351/04, *Ikea Wholesale Ltd v. Commissioners of Customs & Excise* (2007) ECR I-7723, §41.

44. Case 191/82, *FEDIOL v. Commission* (1983) ECR 2913, §26.

45. Case 255/84, *Nachi Fujikoshi v. Council* (1987) ECR 1861, §21.

on the domestic market yield a Normal Value of 8 dollars such that an Export Price of 7, 8 and 9 dollars for comparable products involves dumping as to the sale at 7.

Yes, such calculations require care, and yes, there are many variables. But no, it is not beyond our comprehension. Waiving our role, or limiting it to the formality of notice, timing, deadlines, access to the file, and other procedural errors, weakens the legitimacy of the Union's trade protection measures.

There are examples in the history of both Courts where the Court was very interventionist (such as *Geitling*[46] and *Italian Flat Glass*[47]), and there have been occasions (rather more frequent, though I do not have a precise estimate) where the Court repeated its deference doctrine.

11 EXPERTS

One way of dealing with a sharp debate about the factual reality is to consider experts. In former times, experts were technically skilled persons who could explain sympathetically the physical or mechanical or chemical principles, both in writing and orally. A PhD explained the importance of a supercomputer for his scientific research on the electromagnetic properties of terbium, a rare mineral, in *Control Data v. Commission.*[48] Epidemiologists did the same in *Pfizer Animal*

46. Joined Cases 36, 37, 38-59 and 40-59, *Präsident Ruhrkohlen-Verkaufsgesellschaft mbH, Geitling Ruhrkohlen-Verkaufsgesellschaft mbH, Mausegatt Ruhrkohlen-Verkaufsgesellschaft mbH and I. Nold KG v. High Authority* (1960) ESE 423.

47. Cases T-68/89, T-77/89 and T-78/89, *Società Italiana Vetro SpA and others v. Commission* (1992) ECR II-1403.

48. Case 294/81, *Control Data Belgium NV SA v. Commission* (1983) ECR 911.

Health,[49] where government experts from France and Sweden debated whether it was desirable or necessary or prudent or reckless to prohibit the use of virginiamycin as a feed additive for calves, piglets and turkeys. They served as technically skilled advocates who spoke directly to the judges, always under the control of counsel.

As best I recollect those rather early cases, the written submissions were relatively short and, I stress, intelligible. In recent years, we have seen economist reports of over 100 pages, some with mathematical calculations which I (and maybe others) cannot even read. Sad to say, some econometric submissions are unintelligible and unhelpful pieces of advocacy by zealots who write for other economic experts and not for judges. Clarity, simplicity and intelligibility are elementary elements of advocacy. Obscurity is a bad thing. I have little patience with needless repetition or confident assertions of obviousness before the issue is properly described. I suggest that if a judge finds a report or any other submission too obscure, she may invite the author to supply a five-page abstract or perhaps to agree with the other experts where there is agreement or disagreement. In my tradition it is normal that the judge prefers to be aided by hearing adversaries debate the facts with conflicting expert support. Entrusting (even subcontracting?) the technical questions to a court-appointed expert would be much rarer. But national traditions vary and we can always learn from them.

As a long-term reform, if the current process of decision-making in the Commission cannot be changed, could we have a board of appeal/review panel which could reduce the volume of questions in dispute?

---

49. Case T-13/99, *Pfizer Animal Health SA v. Council* (2002) ECR II-03305.

12 A COMPETITION INTERNAL REVIEW?

The General Court is competent to consider appeals against acts of the institutions, and the specialized agencies which are responsible for a vast range of topics. More than a third of our caseload consists of appeals against trademark decisions of the EUIPO in Alicante. Now, with respect to trademark appeals, the General Court is the third instance of challenge, after an internal revision and after a procedure before a Board of Appeal. The same broadly applies to certain other agencies, including the Plant Variety Office, the Chemicals Agency, the Aviation Safety Agency, the Resolution Mechanism for the Banking Union and the Agency for Railways within which there is a Board of Appeal or Board of Review. The merit of an intermediate layer of appeal is that the issues in dispute undergo a triage. The most important items get clearer and the trivial niggles of subsidiary detail get discarded. Our appeal is better informed, better centred. By contrast, the appeal in a competition case comes to us raw, a vast slab of meaty material into which the Commission (being nervous of judicial review) includes every possibly relevant detail, in a decision, sometimes, of hundreds of pages and hundreds more pages of annexes. It is genuinely difficult to grasp all the implication strengths and weaknesses of such a vast document. Yet the constitutional *need* for a good careful examination is all the more clear (and arguably more necessary) than in the case of a EUIPO decision. And once this Court is faced with such a vast platter, our own judgment is liable to be tempted to deal a dozen minor complications, to the detriment of the two huge points of principle which will set the rules for the future. What about a step between the decision and the Court, such as a board of appeal? The merit would be to help focus the debate upon the biggest issues and separate the question of whether in principle the new doctrine was legally valid from the question of whether the facts justified its application. Would it be too time-consuming? Would it actually reduce the issues and focus them?

The Commission has greatly increased the role of the Hearing Officer in terms of access to the file and preparations for the hearing, but it remains the case that he or she observes and does not decide on whether Mr Smith was or was not present at the cartel meeting. The hearing is not designed to be a trial, but according to the Hearing Officer, the function of determining facts in dispute would make it more *contradictoire*.

Various more fundamental proposals have been mentioned, such as giving this Court a role as a trier of fact, but there seems no serious prospect of such a radical change.

13 A FEW CONCLUDING OBSERVATIONS

There is neither harm nor shame in the annulment by a court of the action of an administration. Nor in the making of a successful *pourvoi* to the Court against a Tribunal decision. No court and no agency gets it perfectly right all the time. There is no disloyalty, no lack of commitment to the goals of the institutions in reversing a decision. That is a psychological question of the necessary mindset. Remember that by rigorous review we enhance legitimacy.

Our judgments sometimes are very long and very defensive. They devote much space to rebutting weak arguments and to subtle questions of admissibility. Their key sentences will often be less than 10% of the total. It would be unfair to present the matter as a binary choice between writing to resist an appeal and writing to inform the litigants. And I certainly do not contend that judgments I have signed have done the one or the other! But we could be simpler. The Commission regards an annulment in Luxembourg as a severe setback, whereas properly viewed it may be 'merely' an indication that the step undertaken was too bold. We ought to be ready to recalibrate our thresholds for when to intervene. And we should be drafting judgments which are clear to the *justiciable*, accessible, simple enough for a non-lawyer to read. Do we really need to record every single *branche* for fear of a *pourvoi*? We should write to inform the most important person: he who will lose.

Oral argument deserves to be used vigorously. The Brits and the Irish brought to Luxembourg in 1973 their affection for oral argument. Instead of a silent, somnolent, respectful hush as counsel read a repetition of the written pleadings, hearings (not always, but often) became a forum for debate, for clarification, for questions as to theories. I urge my colleagues to accept that counsel want nothing better than to know what intellectual problems are troubling the judge. There is nothing rude in disagreeing. There is merit in challenging a doubtful assertion. Preparing to appear before a good appellate court which demands high standards of advocacy is a wholesome stimulus. Let us become more demanding. If counsel has used fifteen minutes to read at high speed a text without contours, let counsel be asked in two minutes to state the three principal points. If counsel are unprepared, on the occasion of their first appearance, they would not be the next time! We should use the mechanism better: there is no merit in tolerating through silence inadequate advocacy. If it is not clear, or irrelevant, or seems to be departing from pertinent rationality, let counsel be guided back to the case at hand. If that tells future counsel that well-prepared advocates have a better reception than others, so be it. The average quality of the advocacy deployed before our Court will improve if we are more demanding.

14 CONFIDENTIALITY CLAIMS

It is my anecdotal impression that claims of confidentiality are made during the administrative proceedings sometimes for good reason and sometimes to kinder comprehension by an adversary. Maybe the same vice afflicts us in Luxembourg. In either case, I suggest we can be robust in refereeing the sport of competing confidentiality claims, which delay much and protect the crown jewels.

15 DISAGREEING WITH THE PUBLIC AUTHORITY

I suggest that it is worth reflecting afresh on the subject of how the Court should proceed when the Commission's decision (Johannes Laitenberger calls it a 'normative choice') lies within its lawful competence and is not vitiated by an obvious procedural error, but yet appears unsound on the merits. Where an agency intervenes on one side or the other where legitimate public interests and private interests compete, the Treaty accords to the Court a set of responsibilities which do not perfectly match the needs of the situation.

16 INTERIM MEASURES

The Commission's power to adopt decisions which imposed an immediate duty to act to conserve a position was established in *Camera Care*.[50] The Court has considered applications for interim measures in many cases, on the great majority of occasions rejecting the application (*Magill*[51] was a celebrated exception, as was *IMS/NDC*;[52] *Microsoft*[53] followed the more typical pattern). I invite us to think of whether interim measures cases might be a convenient vehicle for addressing the problems of delay and of prolixity. An interim measures decision by the Commission can demand, provisionally, a change of behaviour; such a decision can be the subject of an appeal and a parallel request for the suspension of the decision to preserve the *status quo*. This might be a suitable vehicle for testing a novel principle, and indeed there is a pending matter. I speculate that the law might benefit from more frequent use of these mechanisms to facilitate swift analysis, albeit provisional, of the merits of a case. Of course, an interim measures decision by the Commission might be the best way of preventing – in very rare cases – that the marketplace tips in favour of one player. In other, less dramatically urgent situations, the mechanism might help to get a judicial assessment on the issue of principle more quickly.

Our own standards of admissibility for considering judicial interim measures are severe, of course, and I do not underestimate their significance. But I wonder if we might explore interim measures as a means of separating two questions: is the new obligation proposed theoretically available and do the facts justify its imposition?

50. Case 792/79 R, *Camera Care Ltd v. Commission of the European Communities* (1980) ECR 119.

51. *Supra* n. 5.

52. *Supra* n. 7.

53. *Supra* n. 10.

17 AS TO BREXIT

Those who follow competition law should be relatively reassured about the political future notwithstanding the Brexit shock. The UK is an open economy and has well-regarded agencies and well-established judicial review. Cooperation between London and Brussels is close. I cannot imagine that changing. Will there be divergences in particular cases, different points of priority? Quite possibly, in the field of state aids particularly, but there is no structural reason to expect disruption or rivalry, unless the Government were to choose, for reasons of national economic independence, to adopt a directly contrary line. The good Brexit news is the quality of the UK competition authorities.

Brexit politics have been too poisonously confrontational, in which disagreement has been equated with disloyalty, dishonesty and worse. The coarsening of public discourse in my country – and others – must be a dismay for all people of goodwill. I deeply deplore the warlike tones in which negotiations, speeches and dialogues about Brexit mechanics are reported. The UK is not at war with its twenty-seven partners. I heard the new President of the Commission speak after her swearing in, with moderation and read with sadness how that same speech was presented in England as bellicose and inflammatory. There are immense, obvious, real, political and economic challenges which diplomacy must bridge. I urge us all to refrain from presenting these as a prize fight in which the winner knocks out the loser. Diplomats need our encouragement and support not to win, but to resolve a dispute. This is not just a question of aesthetics and good manners, but also a matter of real substance in that voters at war and voters at peace, and their political leaders behave differently.

18 AND FINALLY ...

Finally, it has been an immense honour and pleasure to sit since 2015 with talented colleagues from twenty-seven countries. I have seen fierce debates, impassioned exchange of ideas, the slow emergence of consensus on a text, debates on drafting, and the discussion of novel concepts. At my last conference *plénière* I have seen collegiality, sympathy, generosity, shock, sympathy, solidarity. I had hoped to end my professional career on a high, as a judicial member of this quite fascinating institution. That is not to be. I have no intention of retiring. John Milton, the seventeenth century poet and radical thinker, wrote in *Lycidas*, a melancholy celebration of a deceased friend, a line which might apply:

> At last he rose, and twitched his mantle blue
> Tomorrow to fresh woods and pastures new.

So now I go in search of pastures new. And I look forward to the adventures, challenges, setbacks and successes that competition law can offer those who practise it.

Keeping Geo-blocking Practices in Check: Competition Law and Regulation

Giorgio Monti[*]

1 INTRODUCTION

The creation of a single market has played an important role in the shaping of European Union (EU) competition policy since the early days, complementing EU legislative efforts to remove state-created barriers to the free movement of goods and services. Distribution agreements that forbid or make more difficult cross-border sales are considered particularly damaging.[1] Listen to the Commission's angry tones when condemning Nintendo for entering into vertical agreements to prevent parallel trade of its gaming consoles and cartridges.

* This chapter is based on a presentation given at the GCLC conference in January 2020 and I am grateful for the feedback received then. All errors are mine.

1. *Consten and Grundig v. Commission*, Joined Cases 56 and 58-64, EU:C:1966:41, confirmed in a long line of cases, most recently in *Football Association Premier League and Others v. QC Leisure and Others and Karen Murphy v. Media Protection Services*, Joined Cases C-403/08 and C-429/08, EU:C:2011:631, para. 136.

As a result of these agreements, 'territories are hermetically sealed off, making interpenetrating of national markets impossible, thereby bringing to nought economic integration ... jeopardising a fundamental principle of the Treaty'.[2]

Since the early days this strict approach has been criticized as overly aggressive. First, absent market power up or downstream, it is unlikely that vertical restraints harm competition. Second, even if a restriction on parallel trade restricts competition between two distributors selling the same brand, this should not be a concern so long as there is lively competition between brands.[3] Therefore, even if the agreements set up by Nintendo limit the number of outlets where these consoles may be purchased by limiting cross-border sales, this should not matter from a competition law perspective if Nintendo faces competition from other console manufacturers. With inter-brand competition present, Nintendo's incentive would be to increase output and reduce prices to win market share. As a result, it cannot be assumed that a restriction on parallel trade that disadvantages some distributors will harm competition in the market as a whole.

The passage quoted above serves to explain why these economic arguments have no bite in EU competition law: the Commission takes the view that the disintegration of the internal market, even in the sale of a single product, is a competition harm in itself. This attitude has not changed even after the development of the more economics-based approach to antitrust where more emphasis was placed on analysing

2. *PO Video Games,* Case COMP/35.587 and PO *Nintendo Distribution,* Case COMP/35.706 and *Omega – Nintendo,* Case COMP/36.321 [2003] OJ L255/33 paras 338 and 374 (hereinafter *Nintendo*).

3. Patrick Rey and Thibaut Vergé, *Economics of Vertical Restraints,* in *Handbook of Antitrust Economics* (Paolo Buccirossi ed., Cambridge: MIT Press 2008).

the likely effects of restrictive practices.[4] We thus have a setting where some vertical restraints which fulfil the criteria in the Vertical Block Exemption Regulation are treated in a manner which is in line with mainstream economics and where practices like agreements containing clauses that confer on distributors absolute territorial protection are condemned as restrictions by object without regard to the economics literature.[5]

In 2015 the Commission launched an initiative to complete the digital single market.[6] This led to increased attention being paid to vertical restraints imposed on online trade as well as to a major legislative effort. For the purposes of this chapter, we focus on how EU competition law and EU secondary law have been deployed to address restrictions on parallel trade (often referred to as geo-blocking). This chapter is structured in the following way. In section 2, we review the Commission's re-prioritization towards agreements that partition the internal market. This case law continues an overly strict enforcement against clauses establishing absolute territorial protection for distributors, but it also reveals a procedural innovation: parties who admit an infringement and cooperate with the Commission receive a reduction in the level of the fine. It is argued that this approach is problematic: as will be seen, it is not clear that the agreements that have been challenged are necessarily harming competition. Consequently, undertakings may be tempted by the offer of a reduced penalty and avoid challenging the Commission's hard line against agreements that restrict parallel trade. In

4. *See*, e.g., *Film merchandise*, Case AT. 40433 (30 January 2020), para. 98 (hereinafter *Universal*).

5. To this list one may add selective distribution and resale price maintenance.

6. European Commission, *A Digital Single Market Strategy for Europe*, COM(2015) 192 (final).

section 3, we discuss the Geo-blocking Regulation and not only its role in complementing, but also contradicting the Commission's antitrust enforcement policy. Section 4 concludes by identifying two themes that cut across both regulatory spaces discussed here: the problematic economic grounding of the prohibitions and the responsive manner by which compliance is achieved.

2 GEO-BLOCKING IN COMPETITION LAW

2.1 Substantive Analysis

As a result of prioritizing digital markets in its enforcement, the Commission has issued a number of decisions against undertakings for agreements that serve to prevent distributors from selling outside their territory.[7] In none of these decisions does the Commission assess the market power of the undertaking concerned or inquire as to whether the practices in question harm consumers. This may be justified by dint of well-established case law, but two observations might be made. The first is that if the Commission were to be consistent with the more economics-oriented approach, then it would at least be helpful to select as enforcement priorities those agreements where the undertakings imposing the vertical restraint have market power: this may serve to at least focus enforcement on those vertical restraints where the harm to consumer welfare is more likely to occur. The second is whether the more recent decisional practice of the European Court of Justice (ECJ) requires a more cautious approach to

7. *Guess*, Case AT.40428 (17 December 2018); *Character Merchandise*, Case AT. 40432 (9 July 2019) (hereinafter *Sanrio*); *Ancillary Sports Merchandise*, Case AT.40436 (25 March 2019) (hereinafter *Nike*); *Universal* (*see supra* n. 4); *Meliá (Holiday Pricing)*, Case AT. 40528 (21 February 2020).

challenging geo-blocking agreements, having regard to the types of restraints identified.[8]

On the first point, it may be argued that actions taken against Sanrio and Universal might be justified on the basis of enforcement priority. In these two cases, the undertaking imposed restrictions on parallel trade in the sale of character and film merchandise respectively (e.g., Hello Kitty-themed goods and Jurassic Park toys). It is likely that the relevant market in these instances is brand-specific: a Hello Kitty fan is unlikely to view merchandise with the logo of another character as a substitute. The undertaking's pricing policy likely only affected by the consumer's willingness to pay. It may be argued that there is competition between Sanrio and other firms that make cute merchandise (e.g., Studio Ghibli or Disney) and that Universal competes with the other Hollywood majors in the market for films, so that the commercial popularity of merchandise is the result of competition in a related market, but this does not take away the likely market power that Universal has when selling, say, Harry Potter merchandise. At the same time, if the licensor insists on requiring that the manufacturer/licensee produces merchandise of high quality and its products are monitored by the licensor before being released (as noted in the Sanrio decision) then there may be limited ability for the licensees to compete on price aggressively so that allowing intra-brand competition may not yield significant price reductions for consumers. Thus, the risk of over-enforcement remains even in these instances.

8. *See* generally, G. Monti, *EU Competition Law and the Rule of Reason Revisited*, TILEC Discussion Paper 2020/21 (2020), https://papers.ssrn.com/sol3/papers.cfm?abstract_id=3686619.

On the other hand, it is less clear that Guess (a firm selling clothes and which is struggling against competitors) or Meliá (a firm operating some 300 hotels worldwide) have market power.[9] The *Meliá* decision concerns the relationship between Meliá and tour operators, forbidding the latter from selling to clients residing outside the territory where the tour operator works. Given that tour operators offer a fairly wide range of accommodation other than just Meliá's hotels, the restriction imposed on them is the equivalent of surrendering market share to other hotel chains: when a tour operator is approached by a customer residing in another Member State, the travel agent would be free to sell all other hotels, save those belonging to Meliá. The vertical restraint at play would be problematic if all hotel chains forbade sales outside the territory assigned to a travel agent, but it is not harmful to competition if only one hotel chain forbids it. However, later in the decision the Commission observes that 'vast majority of hotels do not have clauses like this'.[10] In which case this strengthens the argument that the use of this clause harms (if anything) the interests of Meliá, rather than the interests of consumers. It can then be deduced that either Meliá made a commercial miscalculation or that it considers that the restriction allows it to sell more hotels at the expense of its rivals. Remember that you cannot apply competition law paternalistically because you take the view that Meliá would be better off if it allowed sales across borders. Accordingly, absent market power, and absent the parallel use of the same restraint by others, it is hard to discern a theory of harm based on a risk to consumer welfare.

9. *Meliá* (*supra* n. 7), para. 4.

10. *Meliá* (*supra* n. 7), para. 64 – this is in the context of discussing whether the agreement may be exempted, and it is used as a basis for concluding that the agreement is not indispensable.

Moreover, on the facts uncovered it does not appear that all Meliá hotels were distributed with this restriction, which suggests that a proper analysis would also require a definition of relevant markets to see if there is a risk that in certain markets the restraint might have had some anticompetitive effects.[11] The mainstream economic approach suggests that vertical restraints are problematic when we observe either a risk of foreclosure (e.g., an agreement harms or eliminates other tour operators or other hotel chains) or the presence of collusion (e.g., if all major hotel chains implement the same vertical restraint as a way of facilitating anticompetitive practices in the market for hotel rooms). Absent evidence that these risks arise it should be assumed that the contractual restriction is designed to increase the sales the hotel chain can make, e.g., by creating incentives for travel agents to advertise the hotel rather than making easy sales abroad. In sum, a factual setting like the present seems to invite an effects analysis and not a quick condemnation.

One may resist this line of argument by observing that the ECJ has consistently held that agreements that damage market integration are harmful by object.[12] To this, three responses are possible. The first is that the agreement by Meliá does not actually damage the integration of the market for travel operators' services: it only damages the cross-border sales of the rooms in one hotel chain. Is the Commission (and

---

11. *Meliá* (*supra* n. 7), paras 22 and 23 which seem to indicate that about half of the hotels were affected. By analogy, *see Delimitis v. Henninger Bräu*, Case C-234/89, EU:C:1991:91, *SIA Maxima Latvija v. Konkurences padome*, Case C-345/14 EU:C:2015:784, which teach us that a theory of harm based on foreclosure depends on analysing the relevant facts and determining whether the vertical restraints contribute to the foreclosure effect.

12. Another response is that these cases protect the distributor's economic freedom to sell wherever it wants. For reasons of space, this is not pursued here.

the ECJ by ratifying this approach) really serious when finding that the inability to sell one product across borders is an action which harms market integration? The second is that there may be a risk of such a condemnation backfiring: in two instances (*Consten & Grundig* and *Parker Pen*), a manufacturer found to have infringed EU competition law by placing a vertical restraint on its distributor ended up integrating vertically (i.e., buying the distribution side of the business).[13] Absent an agreement, the newly formed vertically integrated undertaking was then free to keep the market segmented. Third, regarding the analytical framework, the ECJ has recently had occasion to reflect on the meaning of restrictions by object and by effect in a number of instances where the conduct had welfare-ambiguous results. At a high level, these judgments suggest that the Court is quite cautious before making a finding that an agreement is restrictive by object. In *Budapest Bank*, the Advocate General advised that in order to determine that a practice is harmful to competition by object one should have regard, among other matters, to experience from the past and economic studies prepared by independent authors that are based on recognized standards as a means of understanding if a given practice merits condemnation by object.[14]

The preponderance of the economic evidence suggests that, absent market power, vertical restraints are benign. In light of this, one option for the ECJ is to refine the object-based approach in the case law by affording the defendant the opportunity to explain why, in light of the relevant legal and economic context, the anticompetitive risks feared by the

13. Giorgio Monti, *EC Competition Law* 41 (Cambridge University Press, 2007).

14. *Gazdasági Versenyhivatal v. Budapest Bank Nyrt. and Others*, C-228/18, EU:C:2019:678.

Commission do not exist. In other words, one could transpose the reasoning of the ECJ in *Intel* to the sphere of Article 101 TFEU. It will be recalled that there, the Court indicated that while the Commission is entitled to make a case based on a formal rule (in that case that exclusivity rebates are in principle an abuse of dominance), the defendant is entitled to challenge this by showing that, on the facts, an anticompetitive effect is unlikely.[15] In this setting then, the Commission, if it still seeks to prohibit the conduct, will have to assess its effects. In the context of agreements containing clauses that offer absolute territorial protection to dealers, there will be instances where the defendants can also show that the restriction of competition is unlikely. The Court could carry out an *Intel*-like readjustment in Article 101 TFEU. In the recent *Canal+* judgment (which concerns licensing agreements that confer absolute territorial protection to broadcasters), the ECJ appears to take this line, indicating that such agreements are restrictive of competition by object, 'unless other circumstances pertaining to their legal and economic context show that they are not likely to produce this result'.[16] This appears to create an opening for the operator of vertical restraints to explain why, on the facts, an agreement granting a distributor absolute territorial protection should not be found to be restrictive absent a close economic assessment.

More radically, the Court could even be invited to depart from its precedents and announce that vertical restraints containing absolute territorial protection are no longer restrictions by object – after all if classification of restrictions by object depends on experience and expert knowledge, then it must be possible for agreements to move out of the object

15. *Intel v. Commission*, Case C-413/14 P, paras 138-140.

16. *Groupe Canal+ SA v. Commission*, C-132/19 P, EU:C:2020:1007, para. 46.

category if subsequent events demonstrate that earlier assumptions are no longer valid.

However, we should concede that the ECJ will be unlikely to follow any of the suggestions above regarding the reinterpretation of Article 101 TFEU and instead hold steady and continue to condemn vertical restraints that are designed to prevent parallel trade. Even so, there are some specific aspects of the recent decisions where the condemnation might have been too hasty. For example, in *Sanrio*, there was a concern that the distributors were required to operate their website using only the language of the territory where the distributor operated.[17] Is this a restriction which may never be tolerated? This appears to be an attempt to avoid distributors make active sales into other territories, which EU competition law may well permit. In *Guess*, there was a concern about the 'exclusive right reserved for Guess Europe to use the Guess brand names and trademarks in online search advertising'. Is this on its own a restriction of competition or is it just a restriction given the overall legal relationship between Guess and its distributors? There is a concern that by adopting decisions where the parties accept all the Commission's findings in exchange for a reduced fine, there is no proper dialogue between the parties and not a sufficient examination by the Commission about clauses that may not always be illegal. On the other hand, these decisions may influence other traders who are likely to use the guidance that emerges from them as a basis for revising their agreements.

17. *Sanrio* (*supra* n. 7), para. 51.

2.2 Settlement Submissions

Procedurally, these recent decisions also embody an innovative approach.[18] While the Commission's leniency and settlement procedures apply only to cartels, the Commission has facilitated a 'settlement submission' policy, which follows closely the settlement procedure for cartels. This allows the parties to obtain a fine reduction if, after the initiation of formal proceedings, they send a formal statement to the Commission wherein they: (i) acknowledge liability of the infringement described in the settlement submission, including an acknowledgement of the facts and the duration of the infringements; (ii) provide an indication of the maximum fine that the undertaking would accept; (iii) confirm that the undertakings have been informed of the Commission's objections and that they have had enough opportunity to make their views known to the Commission; (iv) confirm that the undertakings have been granted access to the Commission's file. In some cases a fifth item is added: confirmation that the undertaking agrees to receive the statement of objections and the decision in a given language, normally English.[19] Upon receiving this submission, the Commission issues a statement of objections which is immediately followed by the addressee reiterating the points made in the settlement submission, which allows the Commission to proceed to a decision, where the fine is capped at the level previously discussed.[20]

18. Its first manifestation seems to be Case AT 39759, *ARA Foreclosure* (20 September 2016).

19. *See*, e.g., *Meliá* (*supra* n. 7), para. 15. The same criteria are found in the Commission Notice on the conduct of settlement procedures [2008] OJ C167/1, amended by [2015] OJ C256/2, para. 20.

20. That there is some discussion about the level of the fine is noted in *Timab Industries*, Case T-456/14, EU:T:2015:296, para. 117.

The result of this procedure is not only a cap on the fine but also a fine reduction. However, it is not clear how the Commission determines what the discount is: in *Guess* the fine was reduced by 50%, in *Nike* by 40% and in *Meliá*, *Sanrio* and *Universal* by 30%. However, there is little in the decisions to explain why the fine reduction differs. The criteria that the Commission applies are similar in each case: (i) acknowledgement of the infringement and provision of additional evidence to the Commission, which serves to strengthen the Commission's case and results in administrative cost-savings for the Commission; (ii) a revision of existing practices as soon as the formal procedures are opened by which the seller provides guidance to its employees on how to ensure compliance with EU Law and changing its agreements with the parties with immediate effect.[21] However this is uneven: in *Meliá* the Commission decision states that the undertaking merely acknowledged the infringement and provided information, no mention is made of a change in conduct, while the parties in *Sanrio* and *Universal* also changed their conduct. The reduction obtained in the *Meliá* case seems excessively generous when compared to the other two decisions.

More generally, further detail is needed to explain why the discount varies, as well as what the maximum discount can be. Of course, the significance of the size of the discount also depends on what level of the fine has been put forward by the parties and how this maximum amount is arrived at between the Commission and the parties. This too could benefit from some elucidation. Moreover, it would be helpful for the Commission to explain the basis upon which the

21. *Universal* (*supra* n. 4), paras 150-152.

discount is larger than in cartel settlements: there the guidelines provide for a maximum discount of 10%, which is largely based on the cost-savings achieved.[22] Here the added factor is that the supplier tries to remove the effects of the infringement by ensuring compliance by its employees and by notifying its contracting parties of the new freedoms they now enjoy: is this sufficient to warrant such relatively generous discounts?

A final puzzle is that in the recent spate of cases the Commission only imposes a fine on the upstream undertaking and not on its distributors. However, the Commission is penalizing firms participating in an agreement, no unilateral conduct. Moreover, in all cases it is clear that the distributors are made aware of what they may and may not do with the contract goods or services. For instance, in *Sanrio* the Commission observed that the seller/licensor intervened in specific cases to prevent cross-border sales having received complaints by other licensees or following a request by a licensee to authorize specific passive sales.[23] The Commission's fining policy in vertical restraints has been patchy in the past as well, frequently imposing a fine only on the supplier.[24] We can contrast the recent case law with the *Nintendo* decision where the Commission also fined the distributors for participating in agreements to prevent parallel trade in gaming consoles, taking the view that it was up to the Commission to determine whether to impose fines on

22. Commission Notice on the conduct of settlement procedures (*supra* n. 19), para. 32.

23. *Sanrio* (*supra* n. 7), paras 39-40.

24. G. Monti, *Anticompetitive Agreements: The Innocent Party's Right to Damages*, 27(3) European Law Review 282 2002, reviewing the early cases. Moreover, the ECJ has also indicated that contracting parties may seek damages against the undertaking setting out the contract terms, rendering matters even more confusing: a party participates in a contract whose effect is harmful to the public interest and the same party is now able to secure damages as a result.

distributors or not. What emerges in the decision is that the distributors not only complied with Nintendo's demands, but also notified it of parallel trade, so that Nintendo could regulate the market. However, this is the conduct found in some of the more recent cases too, and no fine was imposed in these. More generally, one of the distributors in *Nintendo* asked for a fine reduction because of the pressure put upon it by the supplier and because had it not agreed to Nintendo's policy of restricting parallel trade it would have suffered serious harm. The Commission rejected these pleas: the distributor 'should have come to the Commission and complained about [Nintendo's] behaviour, instead of committing the infringement'.[25] On this rationale, it seems unfair that the Commission imposes fines on distributors only selectively: the same concern animating the plea of the distributor above probably applies to most distributors. If vertical restraints are as bad as the Commission believes they are, and if the distributors contribute to segmenting the market, it is hard to justify the failure to penalize these actors systematically.

The choice the Commission made in these recent cases is probably the result of the settlement procedure: since the settlement is made only with the supplier, the Commission would have to start separate procedures against the distributors. Given the case law on hybrid settlements in cartel cases, it would be prudent to run the settlement procedure and the usual infringement procedure simultaneously.[26] This is the approach we see in cartel settlement procedures: there it makes sense to devote scarce resources to pursuing all cartel

25. *Nintendo* (*supra* n. 2), para. 443.

26. *See Icap plc and others v. Commission*, Case T-180/15, EU:T:2017:795, para. 268 noting the importance of protecting the fundamental rights of non-settling parties and how these may be damaged by a settlement decision that includes an evaluation of their conduct.

members, including those who do not cooperate, but in vertical restraints penalizing the ringleader is probably seen as sufficient and the resources needed to issue a decision against each distributor may outweigh the deterrent effect that this yields. Accordingly, while pragmatism explains the Commission's choice to chase only the party initiating the vertical restraints, this comes at the expense of recognizing that frequently distributors are equally responsible for sustaining the practice that is challenged.

3 UNJUSTIFIED GEO-BLOCKING

The Commission did not rest by simply issuing decisions to curtail agreements that harmed market integration. It also proposed a regulation to prohibit certain forms of unilateral conduct by traders which cause harm to the internal market. The Geo-blocking Regulation contains three sets of prohibitions:

(1) Traders cannot deny consumers access to online interfaces (e.g., a user in Belgium must be free to access a *.nl* website: they may not be prevented from accessing the Dutch version nor may they be automatically re-directed to the *.be* site).[27]
(2) Traders cannot apply different conditions of access to goods or services simply based on the nationality or place of resident of the consumer. This means that a consumer has a right to buy goods from traders established in other Member States (e.g., a user in Sweden must be free to order a kitchen utensil from a Spanish trader).[28] However, there is no obligation on the trader to ship the product to Sweden. Another example where this

27. Regulation 2018/302 on addressing unjustified geo-blocking and other forms of discrimination based on customers' nationality, place of residence or place of establishment within the internal market [2018] OJ L 60 I/1, Article 3.

28. *Ibid.*, Article 4.

prohibition applies is when a consumer resident in Germany books a car rental for their holiday in Italy: these consumers must receive the same terms as the consumer resident in Italy making a similar booking.

(3) Traders cannot apply different conditions for payment based on the nationality of the buyer, the place of establishment of the payment service provider or the location of the payment account. Thus, a buyer in Ireland can use a credit card issued by a local bank to buy goods from a trader based in Spain on the same terms as a customer buying with a credit card issued in Spain.[29]

For the purposes of this chapter, four themes are relevant when placing the regulation side-by-side with competition law: the first is that the Regulation prohibits unilateral conduct of non-dominant firms, which is striking when EU competition law seldom imposes such duties; the second is that the Regulation is complemented by competition law (when it comes to copyrighted works), but it also contradicts competition law (when considering online sales). Finally, we observe the possible development of a responsive enforcement style which is analogous to the settlement process discussed above.

3.1 Regulating Unilateral Conduct

From an antitrust perspective, what appears unusual is that the Regulation applies to unilateral conduct without a market power screen and that it also imposes duties to deal with traders, when even under Article 102 TFEU such duties are only imposed in exceptional circumstances.[30] However, there

29. *Ibid.*, Article 5.

30. Pablo Ibáñez Colomo, *The Shaping of EU Competition Law*, Ch. 4 (2018), for a nice discussion of the case law on refusal to deal and how the Commission and the Court have interpreted the scope of Article 102 in this context.

are other instances where duties to deal emerge: a supplier using a system of selective distribution who wishes to benefit from the rule in *Metro* should agree to supply any distributor who is able to show that they are able to comply with all the criteria the supplier specifies.[31] At the same time, this line of case law is best seen as an aberration and for suppliers who benefit from the Vertical Block Exemption Regulation this consideration is irrelevant because the supplier can place a limit on the number of distributors it appoints without losing the benefit of the Regulation.[32]

Much like in the antitrust case law discussed above, the basis for the heavy-handed intervention here seems to be the internal market logic, for which market power is not a relevant consideration. Indeed, the Commission's desire is that 'consumers should be able to "shop like a local" anywhere in the EU'.[33] Another possible explanation for some of the prohibitions is the general duty not to discriminate on the basis of nationality, which is also to be found in the Services Directive.[34] However, under the Services Directive it is possible to offer objective justifications for discriminatory treatment, while the Geo-blocking Regulation affords more limited

31. *Metro SB-Großmärkte v. Commission*, Case 26/76, [1977] ECR 1875.

32. Directive 2006/123/EC on services in the internal market [2006] OJ L376/36, Article 1.

33. Report from the Commission on the first short-term review of the Geo-blocking Regulation COM(2020) 766 (final), p. 2.

34. *See* Commission Staff Working Document with a view to establishing guidance on the application of Article 20(2) of Directive 2006/123/EC on services in the internal market ('the Services Directive') Accompanying the document Communication from the Commission to the European Parliament, the Council, the European Economic and Social Committee and the Committee of the Regions on the implementation of the Services Directive: A partnership for new growth in services 2012-2015, SWD (2012) 146 (final), section 4.2.1.

defences (i.e., the duty to comply with national law or EU Law).

On the other hand, the duties to deal are not particularly onerous: when it comes to sales of goods online, there may be an obligation to sell to consumers residing in other Member States, but there is no duty to arrange for delivery overseas. However, many consumers had expected that they would be able to have the goods delivered to their home.[35] To bridge this gap between what the law requires and what consumers wish for, some entrepreneurs have already emerged to assist cross-border shopping, allowing a consumer to buy in say, Germany, and ask for the goods to be delivered to a warehouse in Germany where the entrepreneur can then collect a bundle of goods and ship them. As these businesses emerge it follows that the trader cannot refuse to make deliveries in their territory even if the delivery address is not that of the final consumer.[36]

The primary target of this Regulation is a firm present in multiple Member States that tends to set different prices for its products depending on the demand conditions of the Member State. The intended beneficiary is the enterprising consumer who, realizing the firm's commercial strategy, shops online to find better deals in other countries. Much like the Commission's antitrust efforts tackles the conduct of multinational firms who use vertical restraints, the Regulation addresses those firms who are vertically integrated in the distribution side of the market.

35. Geo-blocking Report (*supra* n. 33), p. 4.

36. Commission Staff Working Document, First short-term review of the Geo-blocking Regulation, SWD(2020) 294 (final) part 1 of 2, p. 19.

3.2 The Copyright Gap: Competition Law to the Rescue?

The legislator was unable to ensure that the obligations of the Regulation applied to copyrighted works.[37] The matter was hotly debated: in particular given the emergence of online business models, it appeared necessary to extend the internal market logic to copyrighted works. However, as matters stand, viewers in Italy cannot buy a subscription to a film streaming service originating from Finland, unless the Finnish undertaking holds the requisite copyrights in Italy, which is unlikely as copyright owners tend to grant exclusive rights per territory. Absolute territorial protection is inherent in the broadcasting business model, and it is claimed that this model makes the financing of films possible. Nevertheless, this business model has been challenged both under competition law and by the legislator. It is also the reason why the Regulation was reviewed only two years after it was enacted: this would give the EU a second chance to extend its scope.[38]

Insofar as competition law is concerned, three cases allow us to gauge how far licensing agreements that confer absolute territorial protection may be challenged for infringing Article 101. The first case to consider is *Coditel v. Ciné Vog Films*. Ciné Vog was the exclusive cinema distributor for a popular film (Le Boucher) in Belgium. It was also assigned the copyright for the territory. Coditel was a Belgian broadcaster who transmitted the same film on TV from Germany into Belgium.

37. Geo-Blocking Regulation (*supra* n. 27), Article 4(1)(b) excludes 'services the main feature of which is the provision of access to and use of copyright protected works or other protected subject matter, including the selling of copyright protected works or protected subject matter in an intangible form'.

38. Geo-blocking Regulation (*supra* n. 27), Article 9 and statement by the Commission attached to the Regulation.

Ciné Vog brought a damage claim against Coditel claiming that by showing the film on TV this caused it a loss of profits as some consumers likely stayed home to watch the film instead of going to the cinema. The ECJ was consulted twice. It first confirmed that Belgian Law granting Ciné Vog exclusive rights did not infringe EU internal market law as it afforded the copyright holder the right to be remunerated, which was the essential function of copyright.[39] Coditel counterclaimed by arguing that the licensing agreement by which Ciné Vog had been assigned the rights to the film in Belgium created a system of absolute territorial protection which was contrary to Article 101. However, the Court disagreed: it took into account that the essential function of copyright was the ability to show the film multiple times and that absolute territorial protection safeguarded this right. It considered that the territorial protection afforded was limited in time and that this kind of agreement fit well with the business model of film financing. The Court concluded that this agreement was not restrictive of competition by object but that it could be shown that there were anticompetitive effects for example if the exclusive rights were conferred for an excessively long period of time.[40]

In *Murphy,* however, the Court appeared less accommodating to the business model. An agreement between the Football Association and a Greek satellite broadcaster prevented the latter from making available decoder cards for consumers using these overseas. This meant that consumers in the UK would thus only be able to view Premier League football matches if they bought the service from Sky in the UK, which was costlier than the service offered by Nova in

39. *Coditel v. Ciné Vog Films,* Case 262/81, [1982] ECR 3381, para. 14.

40. *Ibid.,* para. 17.

Greece. The Court held that the agreement preventing the passive sales of decoders was a restriction of competition by object.[41] On the facts, this was somewhat of a hollow victory: the defendants in this case were pub landlords who wished to use the decoder card to show live football in their pubs; however, it was found that the retransmission of the broadcast in the UK had a profit-making nature and amounted to a transmission to a new public, i.e., to a group of potential viewers that had not been taken into consideration when the right holders authorized the communication in Greece. Hence, the publican was still in breach of Article 3(1) of the Copyright Directive and could not get away with showing the Football Association Premier League (FAPL) matches using the imported decoders. The judgment thus only protects consumers who use these decoders for private viewing. Subsequent litigation in the UK courts has continued to make parallel trade in decoder cards difficult.[42]

Finally, it was the turn of the Commission to build on the aggressive approach that *Murphy* appeared to open. It investigated the arrangements made by Hollywood majors in the market for pay TV services and issued a commitment decision in *Paramount*, followed by further, similar, decisions.[43] Paramount's licensing model was as follows: it granted an exclusive territorial license per Member State, which was coupled with two obligations: the first was that the licensee (e.g., Sky for the UK or Canal+ in France) would not be able to make

41. Joined Cases C 403/08 and C 429/08, *Football Association Premier League Ltd and Others v. QC Leisure and Others* and *Karen Murphy v. Media Protection Services Ltd*, [2011] ECR I-9083.

42. M. Maduro G. Monti and G. Coelho, *The Geo-Blocking Proposal: Internal Market, Competition Law and Regulatory Aspects*, IP/A/IMCO/2016-14, p. 21 (2017).

43. *Cross-border access to pay TV*, Case AT.40023, 7 March 2019. Paramount made the first commitment in 2016, which is integrated in this decision.

passive sales in other Member States; the second was that the licensor (Paramount) would take steps to prevent licensees from making such passive sales. The Commission considered that these two contract terms were contrary to Article 101 and Paramount agreed not to enforce them and it would not re-introduce them in contract extensions. This was challenged by Canal + , the licensee of Paramount films in France. Commercially, this commitment decision was disadvantageous for it: some French residents might migrate to Sky, reducing the revenues of Canal + . It is true that now Canal + was free to make passive sales in other jurisdictions, but it was unlikely that there would be much demand for its broadcasts, largely for language barriers. Canal + appealed to quash the commitment decision and was successful on a technical point. Recall that the commitment meant that Paramount would not honour its contractual obligation to take action against Sky if it made passive sales into France. This infringed the rights Canal + had under its contract. The ECJ held that the Commission, when issuing a commitment decision was obliged (in order to ensure that it respected the principle of proportionality) to consider the impact of the commitment on the contractual rights of third parties.[44] Here, if Canal + sued Paramount for breach of contract when the latter took no steps to prohibit Sky making passive sales, the national court would be unable to protect the contractual rights of Canal + , given the binding nature of the commitment decision.[45] On the facts, the Court considered that the contractual rights that Canal + sought to assert were 'an essential

44. *Groupe Canal + SA v. Commission*, Case C-132/19 P, EU:C:2020:1007, para. 106.

45. *Ibid.*, para. 110.

element' of the bargain that had been struck between Paramount and Canal + .[46] Therefore, the decision of the Commission emptied the substance of the contractual rights that Canal + was able to assert against Paramount.[47] The judgment is clearly of major importance for the future handling of commitment decisions. However, for the purposes of this chapter, it is but a temporary setback: the Commission can insist that any new contract should not contain clauses that segment the market. Ultimately, the case law supports the Commission's choice to challenge distribution agreements that segment the market even in cases where copyright licensing is involved.

In addition to the application of competition law, some legislative initiatives have begun to erode the assignment of exclusive territories for broadcasts. The Satellite and Cable Directive facilitates cross-border satellite broadcasting and retransmission by cable of television and radio programmes from other Member States.[48] The Portability Regulation allows subscribers residing in one Member State to access their subscriptions to online content when they are temporarily travelling in other Member States.[49]

The Online Television and Radio Programmes Directive covers ancillary online services (i.e., radio programmes, television news and fully financed own productions on the broadcaster) and is designed to facilitate the accessibility of

46. *Ibid.*, para. 126.

47. *Ibid.*, para. 127.

48. Council Directive 93/83/EEC on the coordination of certain rules concerning copyright and rights related to copyright applicable to satellite broadcasting and cable retransmission [1993] OJ L248/15.

49. Regulation 2017/1128 on cross-border portability of online content services in the internal market [2017] OJ L168/1.

these across the EU.[50] All these three legislative instruments implement the country of origin principle, by which the act of communication is 'deemed to occur solely in the Member State in which he broadcasting organisation has its principal establishment'.[51] This allows a broadcaster who has secured the rights to transmit in one Member State to then make that content available across the EU.

The pattern that emerges from these legislative instruments is to find ways of extending the country of origin principle incrementally to facilitate the availability of broadcast content across the EU. However, these interventions are limited in terms of the technologies, the kinds of broadcasts to which it applies, or the duration of the right to access services cross-border. The main reason for the Commission hesitating in proposing a more comprehensive reform is that it is sensitive to the financing model that emerges from the present system of licensing broadcasting rights. This can be observed by considering the substantive arguments in *Canal+* discussed above when it comes to films. Film financing is costly and full of uncertainty: some of the finance for the production of films comes from the broadcaster who then will wish to recoup the cost of the licence by having the exclusive right to broadcast in the Member State. Once retransmission from other Member States is authorized, this would reduce the profits that the broadcaster makes.[52] The concern includes a cultural policy element for the fear that the reduction in film financing would be at the expense of the European film

50. Directive 2019/789 laying down rules on the exercise of copyright and related rights applicable to certain online transmissions of broadcasting organisations and retransmissions of television and radio programmes [2019] OJ L130/82.

51. *Ibid.*, Article 3.

52. *See also* European Commission, First short-term review of the Geo-blocking Regulation SWD(2020) 294 (final) part 2/2, pp. 60-62 and 81-82.

industry and consequently a reduction in cultural diversity.[53] Accordingly, it is unlikely that the Commission will propose an amendment to the Geo-blocking Regulation at this stage: there may be some benefits to consumers but there may be risks to the vitality of the EU film industry which have to be considered too.

However, even with the incremental extension of the country of origin principle in some technologies, the legislation does not prevent contracts that assign exclusive rights, as long as they comply with EU competition law. For example, the Online Television and Radio Broadcasting Directive provides that: 'the country of origin principle should not affect the freedom of rightholders and broadcasting organisations to agree, in compliance with Union law, on limitations, including territorial limitations, to the exploitation of their rights'.[54] In these circumstances, it has been righty suggested that the Commission could intervene with a Block Exemption Regulation to create some safe harbours. If the policy is to safeguard the revenues to finance European film production, for example, then a licence agreement with territorial restrictions that prevent active and passive sales for a specified period of time might serve to strike a balance between the competition considerations and the development of industry.[55]

53. *Canal+ Groupe Canal+ v. Commission*, Case T-873/16, EU:T:2018:904, para. 32. For an excellent assessment, *see* P.B. Hugenholtz and J. Poort, *Film Financing in the Digital Single Market: Challenges to Territoriality*, 51(2) IIC 167 (2020), especially sections 2 and 3 for the commercial context and the predicament of European film makers.

54. Directive 2019/789 (*supra* n. 50), Recital 10.

55. Hugenholtz and Poort (*supra* n. 53), p. 180.

3.3 Vertical Restraints: The Uneasy Relationship Between the Regulation and EU Competition Law

Competition law applies to the distribution contract between the seller and the trader, while the Geo-blocking Regulation applies to the relationship between the trader and the consumer. In general, the two rules apply in a manner that is consistent: in order for a vertical restraint to benefit from the application of the VBER it cannot contain clauses that limit the trader's ability to make sales to any customers or in any territory.[56]

However, the Commission recognized that there may be limited circumstances where it may be useful to allow a seller to impose limits on the trader's ability to make active and/or passive sales in territories outside the one that is allocated to the trader. For example, in case of selective distribution, where the system is organized in such a way that wholesalers are responsible for a set of retail outlets in a given territory, then it may be possible to prevent a wholesaler from making active sales to distributors outside its territory when this prevents free riding on the promotional efforts of other wholesalers.[57] However, passive sales are allowed so a consumer in France may use the website of a retailer in Belgium and order the goods there. Here too, the analysis under competition law and under the Geo-blocking Regulation is consistent.

However, in its competition law analysis, the Commission has taken the view that there may be some exceptional

56. Regulation 330/2010 of 20 April 2010 on the application of Article 101(3) of the Treaty on the Functioning of the European Union to categories of vertical agreements and concerted practices [2010] OJ L102/1, Article 4(b).

57. Commission Guidelines on Vertical Restraints [2010] OJ C 130/1, para. 63.

cases where a manufacturer may prevent traders from making active or passive sales in other territories. First, this may occur in cases where a distributor is the first to sell a new brand or the first to sell a product in a new market, then the producer can take steps to protect the investment made by the distributor by preventing other distributors from making active and passive sales into that territory for two years. Second, if a new product is introduced in a given market for testing, then a ban on active sales outside that territory is allowed for the period necessary to carry out those tests.[58] No decisions have been issued to confirm these two hypotheticals. However, even if these agreements would not infringe Article 101 TFEU, they are automatically void if they infringe the Geo-blocking Regulation. Article 6(2) provides for this result: 'Provisions of agreements imposing obligations on traders, in respect of passive sales ..., to act in violation of the prohibitions laid down in Articles 3, 4 and 5 of this Regulation shall be automatically void.'

Suppose that a manufacturer of widgets, popular in Southern Europe, wishes to take a commercial risk and expand sales to some countries in the Northern Europe. Under competition law, it may enter into agreements with its well-established distributors in the South asking them not to sell in the North actively or passively to allow the new distributor to engage in promotional campaigns there without risking that consumers buy abroad. However, this limitation is not tolerated under the Geo-blocking Regulation because the trader would be in breach of Article 4. This is an undesirable result: the exception from the application of competition law applies in such limited circumstances that it seems unnecessarily harsh to prohibit conduct that occurs only very infrequently.

58. *Ibid.*, paras 61 and 62.

Again, it suggests that the legislator places more importance on the rhetoric that consumers should be free to shop across the EU than to any commercial need of manufacturers. This is particularly so when the exceptions suggested by the Commission apply in settings that appear to actually improve the working of the internal market in the long term by giving commercial incentives to increase the number of countries where goods are sold.

3.4 Enforcement Architecture

A particularly welcome element in this Regulation is the obligation on Member States to appoint an authority responsible for enforcing the prohibitions and obligations to protect consumers.[59] Individual consumers will hardly ever make purchases of such value to justify the cost of litigation, and some infringements may well go unnoticed unless a public authority monitors the conduct of traders. Having said that the maximum fines national authorities may impose differ quite significantly across Member States, ranging from a low of EUR 3,000 to a high of 10% of turnover.[60] This diversity is unhelpful, in particular as traders where fines are at the lower end are unlikely to be deterred. More generally, some have noted that different authorities may place more or less

59. The Regulation also confers rights on businesses, but in some Member States they can only enforce their rights through the courts. Geo-blocking Report (*supra* n. 33), p. 3. This was something the present author insisted on, *see* Maduro, Monti and Coelho (*supra* n. 42).

60. Commission Staff Working Document First short-term review of the Geo-blocking Regulation SWD (2020) 294 (final) part 1 of 2, p. 16.

resources in enforcement. Furthermore, the system contains sufficient incentives to ensure harmonized enforcement.[61]

In addition to a punitive approach to the Regulation, however, the Commission's report indicates that there is a role for persuasion. First, in addition to empowering national authorities (in most cases consumer protection bodies), nearly all Member States have appointed European Consumer Centres (ECCs) as bodies that can offer assistance to consumers (Article 8). The Commission reports that a good number of complaints that have been received by ECCs are resolved amicably.[62] Similar results are obtained when cases go to the authorities where, as of October 2019, there appear to have been no fines issued. The Commission's takeaway from this is that traders need to be made more aware of the obligations that they have under the new Regulation. Another takeaway is that some traders are willing to comply such that the punitive measures foreseen are not helpful in these cases. In the long term, it is expected that national authorities will cooperate via the Consumer Protection Cooperation Framework, which facilitates enforcement for EU-wide infringements of EU consumer law. The evidence to date reveals that this procedure leads to amicable settlements where parties modify their practices to comply.[63]

61. P. Van Cleynenbreugel, *The European Commission's Geo-blocking Proposals and the Future of EU E-Commerce Regulation*, 11(1) Masaryk University Journal of Law and Technology 39, section 3 (2017).

62. Geo-blocking Report (*supra* n. 33), p. 5.

63. Regulation 2017/2394 on cooperation between national authorities responsible for the enforcement of consumer protection laws [2017] OJ L 345/1. Examples of actions taken are reported at: https://ec.europa.eu/info/law/law-topic/consumers/consumer-protection-cooperation-regulation_en.

4 CONCLUSION: LIGHTS AND SHADOWS

4.1 Towards Convergence with the More Economic Approach?

A running theme in this chapter is that trying to stimulate cross-border trade when there is lively inter-brand competition is likely to make a very marginal improvement to competition and to the welfare of consumers. From this perspective, the pursuit of market integration no matter what seems disproportionate. However, neither the court nor the legislator is likely to back down: the image of a European consumer being free to shop anywhere and of traders being free to sell their goods in all of the internal market is too deeply embedded in the narrative of EU consumer and competition law to be shaken by economic arguments.

And yet, we might draw some comfort from the economic assessments carried out by and on behalf of the Commission when examining the pros and cons of extending the scope of the Geo-blocking Regulation to copyrighted works. For instance, in discussing the market for online music the report suggests that most online platforms offer broadly comparable music portfolios in every Member State. There is geo-blocking because suppliers price discriminate to take advantage of different demand conditions, and the prices vary fairly significantly. If geo-blocking is banned, then consumers will in a first instance flock to the cheaper providers. However, there is a concern that since this will harm the profits of the music platforms these may respond either by setting a uniform price across the EU (thus harming the consumers who were able to buy cheaper music subscriptions before) or they might differentiate the music portfolios across states to discourage cross-border purchases. Both of these countermeasures would hurt consumer welfare: studies suggest fairly steep price increases in Member States where prices today are low.[64] Moreover, allowing parallel trade may (even with these countermeasures) reduce the profits of music suppliers: this matters because these firms might then not have incentives to invest.[65] This review thus puts forward a more sophisticated analytical framework to determine whether social welfare would be increased by extending the integration of markets. This is in stark contrast to the more simplistic view that consumers should be free to shop across border for all goods all the time.

Similarly, when it comes to e-books, the evidence suggests that consumer gains from banning geo-blocking are likely to be modest since consumers tend to buy books in their language, so the gains of being able to buy e-books from foreign catalogues are limited. Moreover, the evidence suggests that the compliance costs for small retailers may be greater than the expected gains.[66] Again here, the evidence points away from dictating market integration as a self-evident positive and observing the impact that the facilitation of cross-border trade will have on social welfare, including smaller retailers' larger platforms and cultural diversity.

A similar argument may be made by reference to all kinds of products. A consumer situated in Ireland going online to buy Hungarian handcrafted porcelain benefits greatly from the internal market but a Dutch consumer going on Uniqlo.de

---

64. European Commission, *First short-term review of the Geo-blocking Regulation* SWD(2020) 294 final part 2/2, p. 19. This is the same intuition that was used forty years ago to criticize the approach to price discrimination in United Brands. W. Bishop, *Price Discrimination under Article 86: Political Economy in the European Court*, 44 MLR 282 (1981).

65. Commission (*supra* n. 64), p. 22.

66. Commission (*supra* n. 64), pp. 33-34.

to pay EUR 1 less for the same T-shirt they could buy on Uniqlo.nl is hardly worthy of protection, not least since repeated purchases might serve to raise the price of that T-shirt across the EU as the seller tires to maximize profits. In these contexts, what matters is whether the Dutch price is competitive, something which is ensured by inter-brand competition. Competition law is not to be applied every time a market could be made even more competitive, and definitely not when the market is already workably competitive. We suggest that it is still open for the court to switch to an effects-based analysis for all vertical restraints, so that some agreements that are currently penalized are examined more closely. However, even before this occurs enforcement could at least be prioritized to address firms holding market power.

4.2 Procedural Innovations

While the substantive assessment is less than optimal, a shared element that emerges from the early days of the application of the Geo-blocking Regulation and from the recent practice in antitrust enforcement is the use of a consensual approach to resolving the dispute. This approach is based on the assumption that the parties want to abide by the law and are rewarded for their wish to comply by the application of procedures whereby fines are either avoided (as under the Regulation) or reduced fairly significantly (under competition law). On the positive side, not only is enforcement less costly for the regulator, but compliance occurs more quickly and with a significantly reduced risk of an appeal. Parties willing to comply are also more likely to do so in a manner that is congruous with the aims of the legislation. This is in stark contrast to the slowness of some antitrust cases and where firms at times are slow to comply. Bringing together the possibility to settle amicably (with no fine) or to make a settlement submission (paying a fine but revising one's conduct) creates space for a more responsive form of regulation than relying solely on the deterrent effect of fines.

However, there are also risks: under the Geo-blocking Regulation amicable changes will work well when traders wish to comply but as we noted above the penalties for non-compliance may not be sufficient to deter those determined to infringe the rules. The lesson that emerges from the Commission's use of settlements in vertical restraints as a means of obtaining a speedy change in commercial conduct is that the system needs to be consolidated. First, it is imperative, now that a good number of decisions have been made using this innovative procedure, that the Commission takes stock of its experience and codifies its practice in a soft law document: this will serve it and parties well by rendering the process more transparent and constraining the Commission's discretion. Second, it is also important that undertakings avoid settling and agreeing with the Commission even if at times some of the terms of the agreements are not anticompetitive. The risk otherwise is that, as with commitment decisions, we may end up with a system of prohibitions where novel forms of conduct are neither subject to scrutiny when decisions are made nor tested in the courts.

Territorial Restrictions in EU Competition Law: From *Consten-Grundig* to *Ping* and *Pay-TV*

Pablo Ibáñez Colomo

1 INTRODUCTION

Market integration has a special place in the EU competition law system. Practices that are designed to restrict trade between Member States are, for this very reason, prima facie unlawful, irrespective of their effects, under Articles 101 and 102 TFEU. Thus, agreements that provide for, *inter alia*, export prohibitions,[1] absolute territorial protection,[2] and dual pricing mechanisms[3] are in principle restrictive of competition by their very nature and are, in addition, unlikely to fulfil

1. Case 19/77 *Miller International Schallplaten v. Commission*, EU:C:1978:19.
2. Joined Cases 56/64 and 58/64 *Établissements Consten S.à.R.L. and Grundig-Verkaufs-GmbH v. Commission*, EU:C:1966:41.
3. Joined Cases C-501/06 P, C-513/06 P, C-515/06 P and C-519/06 P *GlaxoSmithKline Services Unlimited v. Commission*, EU:C:2009:610.

the conditions set out in Article 101(3) TFEU.[4] The same is true of unilateral conduct by dominant firms aimed at limiting cross-border exchanges within the EU.[5] The legal status of these practices cannot be explained on economic grounds alone. If only efficiency considerations were relevant in the analysis, the above-mentioned territorial restrictions would not be treated as one of the most egregious violations in EU competition law, only behind cartels.

The special legal status of market integration in the EU competition law system is explained by the place and role of Articles 101 and 102 TFEU in the Treaty as a whole. These two provisions serve, first and foremost, the objective of establishing an internal market within the EU.[6] It is therefore only logical that the Court of Justice (hereinafter, the 'Court' or the 'ECJ') has interpreted them as precluding, in principle, any practice aimed at restoring the very barriers to trade that the EEC Treaty sought to bring down. In the same vein, the Court has consistently held that market integration is an autonomous objective of EU competition law: it is worthy of protection in and of itself. As such, it is not subordinated to the preservation of the competitive process. Thus, a practice may be prohibited even when it is likely to lead to pro-competitive gains (for instance, by injecting and/or intensifying rivalry).

During the formative years of the discipline and up until the early to mid-1990s, restrictions to cross-border trade were a clear enforcement priority for the European Commission (hereinafter, the 'Commission'). A substantial number of

4. European Commission, Guidelines on vertical restraints OJ C130/1, paras 50-54 (2010).

5. *See*, in particular, Joined Cases C-468/06 and C-478/06 *Sot. Lélos kai Sia EE and Others v. GlaxoSmithKline AEVE Farmakeftikon Proïonton*, EU:C:2008:504.

6. European Commission, Protocol (No 27) on the internal market and competition OJ C 115/309 (2008).

cases decided by the authority focused on territorial restrictions.[7] With some rare exceptions, these cases did not raise any novel legal matters and addressed well-trodden questions, such as export bans in agreements for the distribution of goods.[8] As a result of the narrow focus of enforcement, doubts remain about some fundamental issues. Certain of these doubts are methodological in nature: how does the analysis change when market integration is at stake? Other questions are substantive. These include whether there are instances in which territorial restrictions do not amount to a prima facie infringement and whether it is possible for firms to provide evidence showing that a practice is not liable to affect competition.

The primary purpose of this chapter is to shed light on these matters. It appears, in this regard, that the introduction of market integration in a given case has an impact on the way in which restraints are analysed. As a general rule, the analysis of the object of a practice revolves around its precise purpose, and more precisely on whether its aim is anticompetitive. When market integration is at stake, however, the analysis shifts to the means through which the parties seek to attain their goals. As a result of this methodological shift, even practices with a plausible pro-competitive rationale may be deemed to be in breach of Articles 101 and/or 102 TFEU by their very nature.

The observed methodological shift has several consequences in practice, which are considered in the paper. First, doubts may emerge about why and when practices are

7. Pablo Ibáñez Colomo and Andriani Kalintiri, *The Evolution of EU Antitrust Policy: 1966-2017* 83 Modern Law Review 321 (2020).

8. *Ibid. See,* in particular, the comprehensive database that is available alongside the study.

deemed restrictive of competition. The *Ping* case, decided in the UK, shows how the introduction of market integration considerations may create confusion in this regard.[9] Second, the sui generis approach to the assessment of territorial restrictions makes it more difficult to identify the instances in which such practices fall outside the scope of Articles 101 and/or 102 TFEU. This chapter shows, in relation to this question, that firms can escape a finding of infringement by showing that territorial restrictions are objectively necessary to attain a pro-competitive aim. In addition, firms are able to show that the practice is incapable of restricting competition where there are 'insurmountable barriers' to entry within the meaning of *Toshiba*[10] and *Generics*.[11] Finally, while it is in principle possible for a prima facie infringement to be justified under Article 101(3) TFEU (or Article 102 TFEU), the case law and administrative practice are far less clear on these points.

2 WHY TERRITORIAL RESTRICTIONS ARE DIFFERENT

2.1 Territorial Restrictions under Articles 101 and 102 TFEU: An Overview

The single most salient peculiarity of the EU competition law system is the legal status of territorial restrictions. Some of these practices, which are typically subject to a case-by-case assessment of their effects in other systems (including the US

9. *See Ping Europe Ltd v. Competition and Markets Authority* [2020] EWCA Civ 13; and *Ping Europe Ltd v. Competition and Markets Authority* [2018] CAT 13.

10. Case C-373/14 P *Toshiba Corporation v. Commission*, EU:C:2016:26.

11. Case C-307/18 *Generics (UK) Ltd and others v. Competition and Markets Authority*, EU:C:2020:52.

one[12]), are prima facie prohibited under Articles 101 and 102 TFEU. What is more, these territorial restrictions are unlikely to escape the prima facie finding of infringement by justifying them on efficiency or other grounds.[13] The strict treatment of these practices has been consistent even though they have been known, from the outset, to be a source of pro-competitive gains and as such may stimulate rivalry.[14] The mere fact that they are capable to lead to increased inter-brand competition is as such insufficient to justify their negative impact on the intra-brand dimension.[15]

The case law and administrative practice of the Commission give an idea of the sort of conduct that is in principle in breach of the two provisions. Prima facie infringements comprise, first, agreements that give absolute territorial protection to a distributor of goods.[16] In such an instance, the reseller in question would be insulated from sales coming from other distributors as well as from parallel traders buying from the latter. Second, contractual clauses restricting the ability of a reseller to export the contractual goods are also prima facie prohibited under Article 101(1) TFEU.[17] Finally, unilateral practices that seek to limit the ability of resellers to trade across borders amount, in principle, to an abuse of a dominant position. Suffice it to think, for instance, of a dominant

12. For an overview, *see* Louis M Solomon and Robert D Joffe, *Exclusive Distribution and Antitrust* 53 Fordham Law Review 491 (1984).

13. *See supra* n. 4.

14. *See* Opinion of Advocate General Roemer in Joined Cases 56/64 and 58/64 *Établissements Consten S.à.R.L. and Grundig-Verkaufs-GmbH v. Commission*, EU:C:1966:19.

15. *Consten-Grundig, supra* n. 2, 342.

16. *Ibid.*

17. *Miller International, supra* n. 1.

firm that unilaterally limits the amounts supplied to its distributors with a view to restricting exports.[18] The same is true, more generally, of discriminations based on the nationality of the reseller.[19]

Practices that are functionally equivalent to the territorial restrictions described above are also deemed prima facie unlawful irrespective of their effects. This is true, in particular, of conduct that is designed to disincentivise the sale of products across borders. The case law provides several examples in this regard. To begin with, dual price mechanisms, whereby the price for the supply of a product depends on whether it is intended for export, are in principle restrictive by object under Article 101(1) TFEU.[20] According to the *Pierre Fabre* line of case law, the same is true of an outright ban on the sale of products via the Internet.[21] Thus, once a firm appoints a distributor, the latter should in principle be able to have an online presence.

Territorial restrictions that fall short of an export ban or absolute territorial protection are not restrictive of competition by object. In *Nungesser*, for instance, the Court distinguished between a 'closed exclusive licence', which would be prima facie prohibited irrespective of its effects; and an 'open' one, which is not necessarily caught by Article 101(1) TFEU.[22]

18. *Sot. Lélos, supra* n. 5.

19. Case 27/76 *United Brands Company and United Brands Continentaal BV v. Commission*, EU:C:1978:22.

20. *Glaxo Spain, supra* n. 3.

21. Case C-439/09, *Pierre Fabre Dermo-Cosmétique SAS v. Président de l'Autorité de la concurrence and Ministre de l'Économie, de l'Industrie et de l'Emploi* EU:C:2011:649.

22. Case 258/78 *LC Nungesser KG and Kurt Eisele v. Commission*, EU:C:1982:211.

Unlike the former, the latter would not affect third parties' ability to engage in parallel trade. In *Coty*, the Court clarified that a ban on the use of online marketplaces cannot be compared to an outright ban on the use of the Internet by distributors. Accordingly, it is not necessarily restrictive of competition by object, and may fall outside the scope of Article 101(1) TFEU altogether in some circumstances.[23]

These principles find their way in secondary law and related soft law instruments. Block exemption regulations applying to vertical restraints (hereinafter, the 'VBER'), for instance, distinguish between active and passive selling.[24] A similar divide can be observed in the block exemption regulation applying to technology transfer agreements.[25] Whereas limits on active selling is protected by the block exemption (at least in the context of an exclusive distribution agreement), passive sales restrictions are deemed to amount to a 'hardcore restriction' within the meaning of the VBER.[26] The Guidelines on vertical restraints, in turn, express the view – later confirmed by the Court in *Pierre Fabre* – that an online sales ban is, generally speaking, a restriction of passive selling.[27] The same is true of dual pricing mechanisms.[28]

23. Case C-230/16 *Coty Germany GmbH v. Parfümerie Akzente GmbH*, EU:C:2017:941.
24. Guidelines on vertical restraints, *supra* n. 4.
25. Commission Regulation (EU) No 316/2014 of 21 March 2014 on the application of Article 101(3) of the Treaty on the Functioning of the European Union to categories of technology transfer agreements (2014) OJ L 93/17.
26. Article 4 of Commission Regulation (EU) No 330/2010 of 20 April 2010 on the application of Article 101(3) of the Treaty on the Functioning of the European Union to categories of vertical agreements and concerted practices (2010) OJ L 102/1.
27. Guidelines on vertical restraints, *supra* n. 4, para. 52; and *Pierre Fabre*, *supra* n. 21.
28. Guidelines on vertical restraints, *supra* n. 4, para. 64.

2.2 The Special Status of Territorial Restrictions: Rationale and Implications

The rationale for the special status of territorial restrictions was spelled out by the Court in *Consten-Grundig*. This feature of EU competition law is a function of the role of the system in the EU project. The primary objective of the original EEC Treaty was to bring down barriers to trade between Member States, including tariffs, quotas and measures having an equivalent effect. By the same token, competition law is subordinate to the integration of Member States' economies: it is a complement to the provisions dealing with the establishment of an internal market and an instrument to achieve this goal. The subordination of competition law provisions to the internal market was made even more explicit in the Lisbon Treaty.[29]

Against this background, it is not surprising that the Court held, in *Consten-Grundig*, that allowing firms to re-erect the very borders that the Treaty was conceived to bring down would 'frustrate the most fundamental objectives of the [then] Community'.[30] Even though a single distribution agreement is not comparable in its nature and potential effects to legislation restricting trade across borders, the cumulation of agreements or the tolerance vis-à-vis market partitioning can be expected to influence or slow down the integration of Member States' economies. One should note, in addition, that the subordination of competition law to the internal market is

29. Protocol (No 27) on the internal market and competition, *supra* n. 6.

30. *Consten-Grundig*, *supra* n. 2, 340.

not necessarily at odds with the positive outcomes expected from Articles 101 and 102 TFEU. The creation of an internal market is known to be a source of productive and allocative efficiency gains.[31] Insofar as it is, the tension between market integration and the protection of the competitive process relates more to the means used to attain their objectives than to the objectives themselves.

The first fundamental implication of the subordination of competition law to the establishment of the internal market is that the market integration is an autonomous objective of Articles 101 and 102 TFEU. Accordingly, a breach of the said provisions may exist even when anticompetitive effects unlikely to result from the implementation of a practice or when the said practice is unlikely to harm the competitive process and/or consumer welfare.[32] Simply put, a finding of infringement cannot be avoided merely by arguing that the practice in question would not be in breach of Articles 101 and/or 102 TFEU if market integration considerations were not taken into account. Similarly, firms may not argue that the sacrifices from a market integration perspective are immaterial. The second fundamental implication is that the methodological approach to the assessment of restrictions varies when market integration is at stake. In such circumstances, the analysis of restriction changes to focus on the means through which some aims are achieved (and moves away from the latter).

31. European Parliamentary Research Service, *The Cost of Non-Europe in the Single Market: I – Free Movement of Goods* (September 2014 - PE 536.353).

32. *Glaxo Spain*, *supra* n. 3, paras 54-67.

3 TERRITORIAL RESTRICTIONS UNDER ARTICLES 101 AND 102 TFEU

3.1 How Market Integration Considerations Alter the Analysis of Restrictions

The territorial restrictions described above – namely absolute territorial protection and export bans, as well as conduct having an equivalent object and/or effect – would not be prima facie prohibited if the Court's default approach to the evaluation of practices were followed. Thus, conduct that would otherwise be unproblematic may be found to violate Articles 101 and/or 102 TFEU when market integration considerations are introduced in the analysis. Such considerations lead, in other words, to a methodological shift in the assessment of potential infringements. As a result of this methodological shift, the focus of the analysis moves away from the object of the practices to the means through which the said aims are achieved. It makes sense to explain at greater length how the analysis changes.

Under the default approach followed in the case law, the question of whether a practice amounts to a prima facie infringement, irrespective of its effects, depends on whether its object is found to be inherently anticompetitive. Put differently (and to use an expression often found in the Court's case law), the issue revolves around the 'precise purpose' of the conduct under consideration.[33] The analysis of this question hinges, by and large, on whether there is a plausible pro-competitive explanation for it.[34] Thus, where an agreement is capable of having at least ambivalent (both

33. *Ibid.*, para. 55.

34. *Generics*, *supra* n. 11, para. 89.

positive and negative) effects on competition, one can exclude, under the orthodox, default approach, a prima facie finding of infringement.[35] Conversely, where the conduct has no plausible purpose other than the restriction of competition, it would be prohibited irrespective of its effects.[36]

Suffice it to mention three examples to illustrate the operation of the default approach. In *Delimitis*, for instance, the Court considered the 'precise purpose' of exclusive dealing agreements. It noted, in this regard, that single branding obligations serve the interests of both the supplier and the reseller and aligns the incentives of one and the other.[37] Accordingly, the vertical restraint was not found to have as its object, the restriction of competition. In *Asnef-Equifax*, the Court noted that the 'object' (i.e., the 'precise purpose') of credit information exchange systems is not the restriction of competition; in addition, it noted that, by sharing data about the creditworthiness of potential borrowers, such systems may improve the functioning of the markets in which they apply.[38] Finally, in *Groupement des Cartes Bancaires*, the Court concluded that General Court (hereinafter, the 'GC') had erred in law by failing to take into account that the restrictions at stake in the case were a means to address the free riding concerns arising from the features of the relevant market.[39]

35. Case C-228/18 *Gazdasági Versenyhivatal v. Budapest Bank Nyrt. and Others*, EU:C:2020:265.

36. *See*, for instance, Case C-62/86 *AKZO Chemie BV v. Commission*, EU:C:1991:286, para. 71.

37. Case C-234/89 *Stergios Delimitis v. Henninger Bräu AG*, EU:C:1991:91, paras 10-12.

38. Case C-238/05 *Asnef-Equifax and others v. Asociación de Usuarios de Servicios Bancarios (Ausbanc)*, EU:C:2006:734, paras 46-48.

39. Case C-67/13 P *Groupement des Cartes Bancaires (CB) v. Commission*, EU:C:2014:2204, paras 74-75.

When market integration considerations are at stake, the Court departs from this default approach. Instead of focusing on the 'precise purpose' of the practice, the analysis revolves around the means through which the said purpose is achieved. Accordingly, the mere fact that a territorial restriction is a plausible source of pro-competitive gains is insufficient to escape a prima facie finding of infringement. As pointed out above, it was acknowledged from the outset that absolute territorial protection and export prohibitions are capable of having at least ambivalent effects on competition.[40] Still, these restraints were found to infringe EU competition law by their very nature. In this sense, they represent the main departure from the default approach, but not the only one. Resale price maintenance is also known to be a plausible source of pro-competitive gains but is also deemed restrictive of competition by object.[41]

3.2 Escaping a Prima Facie Finding of Infringement: Objective Necessity

Even though absolute territorial protection and export bans are in principle unlawful irrespective of their effects, it is possible for firms applying them to escape the prima facie finding of infringement. There are in essence two ways in which they can do so. To begin with, firms may show that the territorial restrictions are objectively necessary to attain a pro-competitive aim. In this sense, absolute territorial protection and export bans are subject to a higher threshold than other practices. As far as the vast majority of practices are concerned, it is sufficient to show that they are capable of

40. Opinion of Advocate General Roemer in *Consten-Grundig*, *supra* n. 14.

41. Case 243/83 *SA Binon & Cie v. SA Agence et messageries de la presse*, EU:C:1985:284.

having ambivalent effects on competition. When absolute territorial protection and export bans are at stake, on the other hand, it is necessary to establish not only that they relate to a pro-competitive aim but also that the said aim would not have been attained without the said territorial restrictions.

The idea that territorial restraints that are objectively necessary to attain a pro-competitive aim are not prohibited was already present in *Société Technique Minière*. In that case, the Court held that 'it may be doubted' that an agreement amounts to a restriction of competition when it is 'really necessary for the penetration of a new area by an undertaking'.[42] This principle has found its way in the soft law instruments issued by the Commission. In its Guidelines on vertical restraints, for instance, the authority accepts that an agreement limiting both active and passive selling (which is in principle restrictive by object and amounts to a hardcore restriction under Article 4 of the VBER) may be objectively necessary for the parties to attain their aims. As such, it would fall outside the scope of Article 101(1) TFEU in certain circumstances.[43] Territorial restrictions, including export bans or online sales restrictions, may also escape the prima facie prohibition where they are required to comply with the relevant legislation on health and safety.[44]

3.3 Escaping a Finding of Infringement: The Practice Is Incapable of Restricting Competition

There is a second way in which firms may escape a prima facie finding of infringement when market integration

42. Case 56/65 *Société Technique Minière*, EU:C:1966:38, 250.

43. Guidelines on vertical restraints, *supra* n. 4, para. 61.

44. *Ibid.*, para. 60.

considerations are at stake. As the Court held in *T-Mobile*, an agreement must be capable of restricting competition for it to be caught by Article 101(1) TFEU.[45] Similarly, in *Generics*, it confirmed that a finding of abuse under Article 102 TFEU 'presupposes' that the practice is capable of having anticompetitive effects.[46] Accordingly, where a practice is not liable to affect competition, it would fall outside the scope of the prohibition. In such circumstances, the conditions of competition would be the same with and without the practice. By the same token, any alleged effects would not be attributable to the conduct but to other factors pertaining to the economic and legal context.

The Court has confirmed that it is open to firms to escape the prima facie infringement in the context of both Articles 101 and 102 TFEU. In *Murphy*, it expressly held that, while agreements aimed at limiting cross-border trade are prima facie prohibited under Article 101(1) TFEU, it is open to the parties to show why, in the specific economic and legal context of which they are a part, they are incapable of having restrictive effects on competition.[47] In that particular case, the parties had not provided any evidence to this effect. In *Intel*, the Court confirmed that the possibility of doing so is also available in the context of Article 102 TFEU.[48] In addition, it gave precise indications of the sort of evidence firms may put forward to escape the prohibition.[49]

45. Case C-8/08, *T-Mobile Netherlands BV and others v. Raad van bestuur van de Nederlandse Mededingingsautoriteit*, EU:C:2009:343, para. 31.

46. *Generics*, *supra* n. 11, para. 154.

47. Joined Cases C-403/08 and C-429/08 *Football Association Premier League Ltd and Others v. QC Leisure and Others and Karen Murphy v. Media Protection Services Ltd*, EU:C:2011:631 ('*Murphy*'), para. 140.

48. Case C-413/14 P *Intel Corporation Inc v. Commission*, EU:C:2017:632, paras 137-140.

49. *Ibid.*, paras 142-143.

The case law provides additional examples of the instances in which practices are incapable of restricting competition. It is clear, in particular, that the regulatory context may be an obstacle to competition that might otherwise have existed. As the Court held in *Toshiba*, there may be 'insurmountable barriers' precluding competition between the parties to an agreement and thus a finding of infringement.[50] Such barriers may be the consequence, in particular, of intellectual property rights giving a firm the exclusive right to authorise or prohibit certain acts by third parties. The crucial role of intellectual property became apparent in *Generics*. In the case, the Court accepted that a patent may raise 'insurmountable barriers' making actual or potential competition impossible.[51] The instances in which intellectual property rights may preclude cross-border competition are considered in the following section.

4 REMAINING CONTROVERSIES IN PRACTICE

The evaluation of territorial restrictions gives rise to some frictions in practice. This is so for three main reasons. To begin with, there is some tension between the default approach generally followed by the Court to establish a prima facie infringement and the sui generis method applied when market integration considerations are at stake. The duality of methods may lead to confusion in practice, as *Ping* exemplifies. Second, the case law and administrative practice do not provide many illustrations of the instances in which territorial restrictions escape a prima facie finding of infringement. As a result, the conditions under which they fall outside the scope

50. *Toshiba*, *supra* n. 10, paras 40-48.

51. *Generics*, *supra* n. 11, paras 41 and 45-53.

of Articles 101 and/or 102 TFEU remain unclear. Finally, the circumstances in which territorial restrictions may be justified on efficiency or other grounds have never been defined due to the absence of a critical mass of administrative practice addressing the matter.

4.1 The Tension Between the Default and the Sui Generis Approach

The tension between the default and sui generis approaches to the assessment of restrictions is bound to arise in practice. If the territorial restrictions described above are assessed in light of the default approach, the analysis would lead to the conclusion that they are not restrictive by object. The practical difficulty – and the tensions – comes from the fact that the shift in the analysis (from the objective purpose of the practice to the means through which the said purpose is achieved) takes place without being expressly acknowledged by the Court and without it being made explicit. As a result, while the outcome of some judgments may be unproblematic, the reasoning through which this outcome is reached may be at odds with the case law. Similarly, courts and authorities may find it difficult to justify why they reach the result they perceive to be the most reasonable one – or the one that is aligned with the case law – in a given case.

Ping provides a particularly eloquent illustration of this point. Its origins can be traced back to a decision of the UK Competition and Markets Authority (hereinafter, the UK National Competition Authority, or UK NCA).[52] The case concerned the selective distribution system set up by a supplier of

52. Decision of the Competition and Markets Authority of 24 August 2017, *Online sales ban in the golf equipment sector* (Case 50230).

golf equipment. From 2000, the firm implemented a policy on online sales applying to its golf clubs.[53] Sales restrictions regarding the use of the Internet were further refined over the years. Eventually, a 'dynamic face to face' policy – which amounted in effect to an online sales ban – was progressively rolled out between 2007 and 2011.[54] The stated purpose of the policy was not fundamentally different from the one invoked in *Pierre Fabre*. Ping argued that in-person advice and the customisation of its products were at the heart of its sales strategy and brand image.[55]

In line with the principles laid down in *Pierre Fabre*, the UK NCA concluded that the online sales band amounted to a restriction of competition by object within the meaning of Article 101(1) TFEU and its domestic equivalent.[56] The authority's extensive analysis follows faithfully the default approach described above. In fact, it provides for a thorough evaluation of the content of the agreement and its aim in the relevant economic and legal context. The tension between the default approach and the outcome reached in the case became apparent when the UK NCA considered the 'precise purpose' of the clause. Unsurprisingly, the supplier argued that the aim of its distribution policy related to the preservation of its brand image, not the restriction of competition.[57] Crucially, the authority accepted that this was a 'genuinely held commercial concern'.[58]

53. *Ibid.*, paras 3.78-3.101.

54. *Ibid.*

55. *Ibid.*, paras 4.84-4.92.

56. *Ibid.*, paras 4.44-4.82.

57. *Ibid.*, para. 4.88.

58. *Ibid.*, para. 4.99.

However, the decision suggests that these arguments can only be examined as an 'objective justification' that the firm could advance to escape the prima facie prohibition of the online sales ban as a 'by object' infringement.[59] According to this approach, the authority places the burden on the firm to show not only that the territorial restrictions relate to a legitimate aim but also that they are 'suitable and appropriate' to attain the said aim and that they are, in addition, 'necessary'. In this sense, the decision evaluates whether the objectives sought by the supplier could be achieved via less restrictive means and identifies several alternatives to safeguard the firm's brand image that were compatible with an online presence from its distributors.[60]

As would become apparent on appeal, the idea that an agreement only escapes a finding of infringement where there are no less restrictive alternatives is not easy to square with the case law setting out the default approach. The cases encapsulating this approach do not demand an assessment of whether there were other means to achieve the objectives sought by the parties. In *Delimitis*, for instance, the Court did not ponder whether the supplier could have attained its aims by means of conditional rebates, as opposed to outright exclusivity obligations. The fact that such obligations were a credible means to improve the conditions of competition were deemed sufficient to conclude that they were not restrictive by object. This point was confirmed in *Budapest Bank*, where the Court made it clear that the crucial consideration is

59. *Ibid.*, para. 4.83. This approach is reminiscent of the references to objective justification in *Pierre Fabre*, *supra* n. 21.

60. *Ping* decision quoted in footnote 52, at para. 4.96.

whether the agreement is capable of having ambivalent effects on competition.[61]

It is against this background that the Competition Appeal Tribunal (hereinafter, the 'CAT') reviewed the legality of the *Ping* decision. Even though it did not dispute the outcome reached in it, the analysis departed in several respects from that undertaken by the authority. In particular, it noted that the proportionality analysis that the authority had undertaken was not appropriate to determine whether an agreement amounts to a restriction by object. In this regard, the CAT concluded that the decision had conflated two separate issues: the objective necessity test as described above (which would lead to the conclusion that the agreement falls outside the scope of the prohibition altogether) and the evaluation of the object of the agreement.[62] By conflating the two issues, the UK NCA had suggested that an agreement would infringe Article 101(1) TFEU by object unless it is shown to be objectively necessary.

The analysis performed by the CAT was, however, also at odds with the case law in two respects. To begin with, it departed from the default approach as described above in a number of ways. In particular, the CAT did not accept that the fundamental question under the default approach is whether an agreement is capable of having ambivalent effects on competition. Even though *Delimitis* provides a clear example of how the evaluation is to be conducted in practice, the tribunal denied its relevance in the specific context of the *Ping* case.[63] The CAT also suggested that 'crisis cartels', such as the

61. *Budapest Bank*, *supra* n. 35, paras 82-83.

62. *Ping Europe Ltd v. Competition and Markets Authority* [2018] CAT 13, paras 97-100.

63. *Ibid.*, para. 104.

one at stake in *BIDS*,[64] have a plausible pro-competitive justification.[65] The review tribunal reached this conclusion despite the fact that the distinctive feature of cartel arrangements is precisely the lack of redeeming virtues.[66]

Second, the CAT judgment appears to conflate the object of the agreement and the means through which the said object is achieved. As a result, it comes across as somewhat contradictory. On the one hand, the judgment concluded that the precise purpose of the agreement is to restrict the sale of golf equipment over the Internet.[67] On the other hand, it seemingly accepted that the territorial restrictions pursue a legitimate aim, relating to the promotion of custom fittings.[68] This internal contradiction would have been avoided if the Court had simply acknowledged that, even when the object of a practice is not inherently anticompetitive, there are means to attain a legitimate aim that are restrictive by their very nature. In this regard, the tribunal does not engage with the question of why online sales bans amount to a 'by object' infringement, even though they relate to a legitimate aim.

In January 2020, the Court of Appeal dismissed the challenge brought by Ping against the CAT ruling.[69] The judgment is notable in that it was delivered after AG Bobek's Opinion in *Budapest Bank*.[70] This Opinion confirmed the principles underpinning the default approach as described

64. Case C-209/07 *Competition Authority v. Beef Industry Development Society Ltd and Barry Brothers (Carrigmore) Meats Ltd*, EU:C:2008:643.

65. *Ibid.*, para. 101.

66. *Cartes Bancaires*, *supra* n. 39, para. 51; and *Budapest Bank*, *supra* n. 35, para. 36.

67. *Ping Europe Ltd v. Competition and Markets Authority* [2018] CAT 13, para. 159.

68. *Ibid.*, paras 147 and 162.

69. *Ping Europe Ltd v. Competition and Markets Authority* [2020] EWCA Civ 13.

70. Opinion of AG Bobek in Case C-228/18 *Gazdasági Versenyhivatal v. Budapest Bank Nyrt. and Others*, EU:C:2019:678.

above. In particular, AG Bobek emphasised that agreements with a plausible pro-competitive rationale are not restrictive by their very nature. Because the Court of Appeal delivered its judgment before the *Budapest Bank* ruling was issued, Lady Justice Rose questioned whether the AG Bobek's Opinion truly captured the essence of the default approach and questioned whether the Court of Justice would follow it.[71] In addition, it hinted at the fact that *Cartes Bancaires*, on which Ping relied, concerned a particular economic and legal context the peculiarities of which – namely the two-sided nature of the market – were not present in the case at hand.[72]

The Court of Appeal, in other words, denied the relevance of the default approach to uphold the outcome in *Ping* – that the outright ban on online sales is restrictive of competition by object. The judgment in *Budapest Bank*, delivered shortly afterwards, reveals the ways in which its analysis departed from the logic underpinning the case law. On the other hand, the Court of Appeal failed to advance an alternative rationale justifying the outcome it reached. In this sense, the judgment illustrates how national courts may struggle when making sense of, and upholding, the relatively stricter stance vis-à-vis territorial restrictions that go against market integration. If anything, the appeal judgment in *Ping* is remarkable for the conspicuous absence of market integration in the assessment. Simply noting that outright bans on online sales amount, by their very nature, to a restriction of passive sales and as such go against cross-border trade would have allowed the Court of Appeal to reach the desired – and uncontroversial – outcome. It would also have provided the rationale that it failed to offer.

71. *Ibid.*, para. 102.

72. *Ibid.*

4.2 Escaping a Prima Facie Infringement in Practice

As explained above, territorial restrictions going against market integration can escape a prima facie finding of infringement in two circumstances: where they meet the objective necessity test and where they are incapable of restricting competition in the economic and legal context in which they are implemented. However, the case law and administrative practice do not provide a wealth of examples shedding light on the practical implementation of these principles. As a result, doubts remain about when and why territorial restrictions fall outside the scope of Article 101(1) TFEU altogether. Crucially, some of the most recent administrative practice by the Commission has explored the instances in which cross-border restraints might not amount to a 'by object' infringement.

To begin with, an agreement may be incapable of restricting competition where there are 'insurmountable barriers to entry'. As pointed out above, scenarios where intellectual property is at stake provide the most frequent and obvious examples of instances in which territorial restrictions may not be capable of restricting competition that might otherwise have existed. As a matter of principle, intellectual property rights are not an 'insurmountable barriers' to cross-border trade within the EU. This is so because the exhaustion doctrine applies at the level of the EEA as a whole. Accordingly, once a product is sold within the EEA by the right holder or with its consent, it can circulate freely across EU borders.[73] Thus, a right holder or a licensee cannot invoke intellectual rights to prevent cross-border trade. This is the scenario at

73. Case 78/70 *Deutsche Grammophon*, EU:C:1971:59; Case 16/74 *Centrafarm BV and Adriaan de Peijper v. Winthrop BV*, EU:C:1974:115; and Case 15/74 *Centrafarm BV and Adriaan de Peijper v. Sterling Drug Inc*, EU:C:1974:114.

stake in *Consten-Grundig*[74] and *Nungesser.*[75] Because the products had been sold with the consent of the right holder in these two cases, clauses providing for absolute territorial protection were found to be prima facie unlawful.

Secondary legislation may also bring down barriers that would otherwise have been 'insurmountable'. One example is the so-called SatCab Directive, which introduced the 'country of origin' principle for broadcasting via satellite.[76] In accordance with this principle, the satellite broadcast is deemed to occur solely in the Member State in which the transmission originates.[77] As a consequence, licensees in different Member States can compete with each other for the same viewers without infringing their respective rights. This is the factual scenario at the origin of *Murphy*. Because the underlying intellectual property regime was not an 'insurmountable barrier' to cross-border transmissions, the 'additional obligations' limiting the ability of a Greek broadcaster to offer its services to UK viewers were found to be restrictive of competition by object.[78]

Conversely, there may be instances where a right holder may validly invoke its intellectual property rights to prevent cross-border trade. In these instances, such rights become an 'insurmountable barrier'. First, one can think of an instance in

74. *Consten-Grundig, supra* n. 2.

75. *Nungesser, supra* n. 22.

76. Council Directive 93/83/EEC of 27 September 1993 on the coordination of certain rules concerning copyright and rights related to copyright applicable to satellite broadcasting and cable retransmission OJ (1993) L 248/15.

77. In accordance with Article 1(2)(b) of the Directive, '[t]he act of communication to the public by satellite occurs solely in the Member State where, under the control and responsibility of the broadcasting organization, the programme-carrying signals are introduced into an uninterrupted chain of communication leading to the satellite and down towards the earth'.

78. *Murphy, supra* n. 47, paras 134-146.

which there is no exhaustion insofar as products have not been put on the market by the right holder or with its consent. For instance, it may be that there are no economic links between two producers using the same trademark in two different Member States.[79] In such circumstances, the producer in one country may oppose the import of goods manufactured by an unaffiliated producer and originating in another country. Allowing the two products to co-exist in a given market would jeopardise the essential function of trademarks, which, according to the case law, is to 'guarantee the identity of origin' of the goods in question.[80]

Second, there may be instances in which the intellectual property right is not subject to exhaustion. In such cases, the right holder and its licensees would be in a position to prevent cross-border trade. For the same reason, agreements limiting such trade would not be capable of restricting competition. Even in their absence, cross-border competition would have been precluded by the underlying regulatory framework. This conclusion is apparent when one considers *Coditel II*.[81] That case concerned a licensing agreement giving absolute territorial protection in a Member State. Because the intellectual property right was not subject to exhaustion,[82] the licensee was in a position to prohibit licensees based in other Member States from offering the licensed content in its exclusive territory. The Court ruled that, in and of itself, the licensing

79. *See* Case C-9/93 *IHT Internationale Heiztechnik GmbH and Uwe Danzinger v. Ideal-Standard GmbH and Wabco Standard GmbH*, EU:C:1994:261; and Case C-291/16 *Schweppes SA v. Red Paralela SL and Red Paralela BCN SL*, EU:C:2017:990.

80. C-10/89 *SA CNL-SUCAL NV v. HAG GF AG*, EU:C:1990:359, para. 14.

81. Case 262/81 *Coditel SA, Compagnie générale pour la diffusion de la télévision, and others v. Ciné-Vog Films SA and others*, EU:C:1982:334.

82. Case 62/79 *SA Compagnie générale pour la diffusion de la télévision, Coditel, and others v. Ciné Vog Films and others*, EU:C:1980:84.

agreement does not violate Article 101(1) TFEU.[83] Accordingly, any restrictive effects would not result from the absence of competition from other distributors, but from other factors.[84]

4.2.1 *Case Study 1:* Character Merchandise (Sanrio)

The Commission has been confronted with these scenarios in its recent administrative practice. In *Character Merchandise*, it considered the lawfulness of the restrictions imposed by Sanrio on its licensees in the EU.[85] As in *Nungesser*, the licences covered the manufacturing and the distribution of the products.[86] The Commission raised concerns about clauses limiting the licensees' ability to engage in active and passive selling outside the territory covered by the agreement.[87] In addition to the outright bans on active and passive selling, some clauses expressly prohibited online sales (altogether or outside the territory covered by the licence),[88] required the licensee to refer orders from other territories[89] and limited the languages that it could use for the sale of its products.[90]

83. *Coditel II*, *supra* n. 8, para. 15.

84. *Ibid.*, para. 19: 'It must therefore be stated that it is for national courts, where appropriate, to make such inquiries and in particular to establish whether or not the exercise of the exclusive right to exhibit a cinematographic film creates barriers which are artificial and unjustifiable in terms of the needs of the cinematographic industry, or the possibility of charging fees which exceed a fair return on investment, or an exclusivity the duration of which is disproportionate to those requirements, and whether or not, from a general point of view, such exercise within a given geographic area is such as to prevent, restrict or distort competition within the common market.'

85. Commission Decision of 9 July 2019 in Case AT. 40432 – *Character Merchandise*.

86. *Ibid.*, paras 16-30.

87. *Ibid.*, paras 31-58.

88. *Ibid.*, paras 45-48.

89. *Ibid.*, paras 49-50.

90. *Ibid.*, paras 51-52.

The analysis of some of these clauses is straightforward. Since the licences covered the manufacturing and sale of the licensed goods, and since the goods were produced with Sanrio's consent, the licensees in the different territories were not in a position to invoke their rights to prevent cross-border trade. In other words, Sanrio's intellectual property rights were not an 'insurmountable barrier' to active and passive selling across borders. By the same token, the finding that outright bans on online and/or passive selling amount to a restriction of competition by object comes across as straightforward and uncontroversial. The interest of the decision lies elsewhere. There are at least two issues that are not immediately obvious to reconcile with the conclusions drawn from the discussion above.

First, the Commission argues in the decision that the status of territorial restrictions as 'by object' infringements does not depend on whether the intellectual property rights are exhausted.[91] According to this view, there would be a prima facie infringement of Article 101(1) TFEU even when a right holder or a licensee would be able to validly invoke its intellectual property to prevent imports. Put differently, the Commission argued that a restriction by object may exist even when an agreement is incapable of restricting competition. This position is difficult to square with the Court's judgment in *Generics*, which makes it clear that there would be no restriction, whether by object or effect, where there are 'insurmountable barriers' to actual or potential competition.

91. *Ibid.*, para. 62: 'The Commission finds that the practices investigated in this case, including the restrictive clauses in agreements for the licensing and distribution of merchandise products, amount to restrictions prohibiting or limiting the cross-border supply of goods. Irrespective of whether intellectual property rights are exhausted, such restrictions fall under Union competition law.'

A second notable aspect of the decision has to do with its position in relation to active sales restrictions. The Commission treats such restrictions as 'by object' infringements. This is so even though, as mentioned above, they are not deemed to amount to a 'hardcore restriction' within the meaning of Article 101(1) TFEU when imposed in the context of an exclusive distribution agreement. This expansive interpretation of the notion of restriction of competition by object suggests that there may be territorial restraints other than absolute territorial protection and export bans that amount to a prima facie infringement. However, the decision fails to identify a precedent providing direct support for the proposition that active sales restrictions amount to a 'by object' infringement.[92] It simply cites *Consten-Grundig*, a case that concerned absolute territorial protection.

One can think of several reasons why the Commission's expansive interpretation of Article 101(1) TFEU is not wholly uncontroversial. The authority's position would imply that all forms of territorial protection are in principle restrictive by object. This position cannot be easily reconciled with *Société Technique Minière*. In that ruling, the Court held that the legality of territorial restrictions demands a case-specific inquiry shedding light on its object and/or effect. In this sense, it noted, in particular, that the lawfulness of such restraints depends, at least in part, on the 'severity' of the clauses providing for territorial protection.[93] One could therefore reasonably argue that a limitation on active selling, which does not preclude or limit parallel trade and/or passive sales,

92. *Ibid.*, para. 77.

93. *Société Technique Minière*, *supra* n. 42, 250.

demands a case-by-case analysis of its effects.[94] What is more, *Nungesser* – with the divide between 'open' and 'closed' licences – supports this same conclusion. In *Character Merchandise*, the Commission fails to engage with these two key precedents altogether. The latter seemed particularly relevant, as it concerned a similar licensing arrangement.

4.2.2 Case Study 2: **Pay-TV**

In *Pay-TV*, the Commission examined the lawfulness of some clauses concluded in the licensing agreements between Sky UK, a broadcaster providing subscription-based services, and the Hollywood major studios.[95] The single most interesting aspect of this case related to the clauses limiting Sky UK's ability to offer, online, the licensed content outside the territory covered by the agreement.[96] According to the concerns justifying the opening of the investigation, these restraints limited passive sales and as such could amount to a restriction of competition by object.[97] The case was closed following the commitments offered by the Hollywood major studios, which agreed not to introduce similar obligations in the future and not to honour or enforce obligations limiting passive selling in existing agreements (with Sky UK and with licensees based in other territories within the EEA).[98] The commitment decision offered by one of the studios was challenged by another

94. *The EU Law of Competition* 9.09 (Jonathan Faull and Ali Nikpay ed., 3rd edn, Oxford University Press 2014).

95. *See*, in particular, Commission Decision of 26 July 2016 in Case AT.40023 – *Cross-border access to pay-TV* (hereinafter, the '*Paramount* Decision').

96. *Ibid.*, paras 28-30.

97. *Ibid.*, paras 31-44.

98. *See*, in this sense, Commission Decision of 7 March 2019 in Case AT.40023 – *Cross-border access to pay-TV*.

licensee – Canal + .[99] This decision was annulled by the Court in December 2020.[100]

Because the Commission did not adopt an infringement decision, the qualification of the above-mentioned clauses as a prima facie infringement of Article 101(1) TFEU did not go beyond a preliminary assessment. This, in fact, is one of the points emphasised by the Court in its *Canal+* ruling.[101] Since the analysis was insufficiently deep and failed to consider all aspects pertaining to the economic and legal context of which the clauses were a part, the Commission failed to addressed key questions. The single most conspicuous absence from the preliminary assessment was the operation of the copyright regime, and its implications for the provision of services across borders. This question is all the more relevant following the Court's ruling in *Generics*.

In accordance with Article 3(1) of the so-called InfoSoc Directive, authors have the exclusive right or prohibit any 'communication to the public', including the 'making available to the public of their works'.[102] Crucially, Article 3(3) clarifies that this right is not subject to exhaustion.[103] The fundamental consequence is that the authorisation of the author is required for every act of communication to the public or making available to the public. In this sense, the regulatory context in *Pay-TV* is not fundamentally different

99. Case T-873/16 *Groupe Canal+ SA v. Commission*, EU:T:2018:904.

100. Case C-132/19 P *Groupe Canal+ SA v. Commission*, EU:C:2020:1007.

101. *Ibid.*, para. 54.

102. Directive 2001/29/EC of the European Parliament and of the Council of 22 May 2001 on the harmonisation of certain aspects of copyright and related rights in the information society OJ (2001) L 167/10.

103. In accordance with Article 3(3) of the Directive 'The rights referred to in paragraphs 1 and 2 shall not be exhausted by any act of communication to the public or making available to the public as set out in this Article.'

from that at stake in *Coditel II*. On the other hand, the case is different from *Murphy* in a second key respect. Unlike the latter, the cross-border provision of online content, to the extent that it is subject to the InfoSoc Directive, demands a licence in the 'country of destination' of the transmission.[104]

Against this background, the fundamental question that emerges in *Pay-TV* is whether the copyright regime raised an 'insurmountable barrier' to the transmission of online content in territories other than the one covered by the licence. Contrary to what was true in *Generics*, it would seem that the validity of the copyright is not at stake in the case. Because the 'country of destination' principle is applicable, moreover, it is difficult to avoid the conclusion that transmitting services across territories would amount to a copyright infringement. By the same token, any absence of cross-border competition would be attributable to the intellectual property regime and not to the contentious clauses. The said clauses, in other words, would not be capable of restricting actual or potential competition that would have existed in their absence. Because they are incapable of restricting competition their object cannot be anticompetitive. By definition, their precise purpose has to be a different one.

If one accepts that the copyright regime raises an 'insurmountable barrier' to the cross-border provision of online content, the question that emerges is that of why the clauses were introduced in the agreements in the first place. Assuming that the transmissions would have been unlawful, it is necessary to offer an explanation of why the various licensors felt the need to include such clauses in their agreements. One

104. For an analysis of the question, *see* Justin Koo, *The Right of Communication to the Public in EU Copyright Law* Chapter 6 (Hart Publishing 2019); and Commission Report on the first short-term review of the Geo-blocking Regulation COM(2020) 766 final, 10-12.

could argue, in line with *Generics*, that the very inclusion of the clauses is an indicator that the licensees in the various territories were at least potential competitors.[105] Among the several potential explanations for the inclusion of the clauses, one should consider the difficulty of detecting copyright infringements over the internet and taking prompt action against them. From this perspective, they could be seen as additional obligations aimed at reducing the transaction costs involved in the respect of the terms under which the rights are licensed. The object of reducing transaction costs is not unusual in copyright licensing agreements. In *Tournier*, for instance, the Court accepted that horizontal price-fixing may be a necessary mechanism to allow authors to meaningfully exploit their copyright.[106]

4.3. The Application of Article 101(3) TFEU to Territorial Restrictions

A third area in which the case law and administrative practice provide insufficient guidance relates to the application of Article 101(3) TFEU. The Court has consistently held that agreements that are prohibited under Article 101(1) TFEU may fulfil the conditions set out in the third paragraph. It is immaterial, in this regard, whether they are 'by object' or 'by effect' infringements.[107] Thus, even though the former are particularly egregious breaches of EU competition law, they can escape the prohibition where the parties can show that the conditions set out in Article 101(3) TFEU are fulfilled. In fact, territorial restrictions are particularly suitable for an

105. *Generics, supra* n. 11, para. 55.

106. Case 395/87 *Ministère public v. Jean-Louis Tournier*, EU:C:1989:319, para. 31.

107. *Glaxo Spain, supra* n. 3, paras 78-88.

exemption under the said provision. Unlike cartels, which lack redeeming virtues, absolute territorial protection and export bans are known to be a source of efficiency gains. They therefore have the potential to fulfil the first condition of Article 101(3) TFEU (which is the hurdle that cartel arrangements are, by definition, unable to overcome).[108]

As a matter of principle, the Commission is ready to accept the idea that absolute territorial protection, export bans and measures having an equivalent effect can be exempted in certain circumstances. It has been explained above that, in its Guidelines on vertical restraints, the authority goes as far as to acknowledge that shielding a distributor from active and passive selling may fall outside the scope of Article 101(1) TFEU altogether on account of the pro-competitive gains resulting from the agreement.[109] In the same vein, it explains that there are instances in which a dual pricing mechanism penalising, in effect, online sales, may be justified under Article 101(3) TFEU.[110]

In practice, however, the Commission has not adopted a decision declaring that an agreement fulfils the conditions set out in Article 101(3) TFEU. This is true across the board, in the sense that it is not limited to territorial restrictions. In the years since the adoption of Regulation 1/2003, the Commission has not adopted a 'finding of inapplicability' decision concluding that Articles 101 and/or 102 TFEU are not infringed.[111] In the specific context of territorial restrictions, the

108. Guidelines on vertical restraints, *supra* n. 4, paras 107-109.

109. *Ibid.*

110. *Ibid.*, para. 64.

111. *See*, in this sense, Ibáñez Colomo and Kalintiri, *supra* n. 7; and Jacques Buhart and David Henry, *COVID-20: The Comfort Letter Is Dead. Long Live the Comfort Letter?* 43 World Competition 305 (2020).

parsimony with which these decisions are adopted is perhaps best exemplified by the aftermath of *Glaxo Spain*.[112] This case concerned a dual price mechanism such as the one described above, and this in a specific economic and legal context – the pharmaceutical industry.

Glaxo Spain was uneventful from the perspective of the application of Article 101(1) TFEU. The Court found that the dual pricing mechanism amounted to a restriction of competition by object, and this on account on the fact that it had been designed to discourage exports.[113] On the other hand, the judgment on appeal concurred with the first instance judgment in finding that the Commission's analysis under Article 101(3) TFEU was insufficiently motivated. In particular, the Court concluded that the GC had not erred when finding that the authority had failed to evaluate whether the dual pricing mechanism was likely to lead to efficiency gains.[114] Both the Court and the GC judgments left the door open to the application of Article 101(3) TFEU. At the very least, they suggested that the arguments advanced in favour of territorial restrictions deserve to be taken seriously and cannot be simply brushed aside.

Against this background, the aftermath of the case provided a good occasion for the Commission to identify the circumstances in which dual pricing mechanisms (and, more generally, parallel trade restrictions) can be justified under Article 101(3) TFEU. Arguably, the need for guidance in this respect was particularly needed in the pharmaceutical sector,

112. Case T-574/14 *European Association of Euro-Pharmaceutical Companies (EAEPC) v. Commission*, EU:T:2018:605.

113. Commission Decision 2001/791/EC of 8 May 2001 in Cases IV/36.957/F3 *Glaxo Wellcome*, IV/36.997/F3 *Aseprofar and Fedifar*, IV/37.121/F3 *Spain Pharma*, IV/37.138/F3 BAI and IV/37.380/F3 *EAEPC* OJ (2001) L 302/1.

114. *Glaxo Spain*, *supra* n. 3, para. 81.

which has some peculiarities that, according to some stakeholders, would justify the sort of territorial restraints that would be unacceptable in other circumstances. It has been argued, in this sense, that accepting parallel trade in the pharmaceutical sector amounts, in effect, to exporting the regulatory choices made in the exporting Member State to the importing one.[115] According to this view – and given how crucial regulation is in determining the prices of medicines – it would not be a sector like the others.

Glaxo Spain provided two openings to engage with the application of Article 101(3) TFEU. First, a complainant in the case invited the authority to adopt a decision reinstating the finding that the dual pricing strategies amount to a breach of Article 101(1) TFEU that cannot be justified. However, the Commission rejected this complaint on grounds of lack of Union interest.[116] It argued that the behaviour had ceased and that there had been no persistent effects as a result of the implementation of the practice.[117] The GC, in turn, dismissed the challenge against the rejection decision.[118] Second, the Commission opened an investigation into the dual pricing strategies, similar to those at stake in *Glaxo Spain*, and allegedly implemented by pharmaceutical companies other than GlaxoSmithKline.[119] This investigation, however, was closed without the adoption of a decision.

115. *See* in this sense, for a discussion, Patrick Rey and James S Venit, *Parallel Trade of Prescription Medicines: The Glaxo Dual Pricing Case* in *Cases in European Competition Policy – The Economic Analysis* (Bruce Lyons ed., Cambridge University Press 2012).

116. Commission Decision of 27 May 2014 in Case AT.36957 – *Glaxo Wellcome*.

117. *Ibid.*, para. 23.

118. *EAEPC*, *supra* n. 112.

119. Case AT.39973 – *Pricing schemes for distribution of medicines in Spain*.

5 CONCLUSIONS

Almost sixty years have passed since the seminal rulings in *Société Technique Minière* and *Consten-Grundig*. The vast case law and administrative practice issued since then have clarified, beyond doubt, a number of matters on the status of territorial restrictions under Articles 101 and 102 TFEU. The Court has consistently held that market integration is an autonomous objective of the EU competition law system, in the sense that it is worthy of protection in and of itself. Accordingly, some practices that would otherwise be unproblematic can be found to be in breach of Articles 101 and/or 102 TFEU. The range of practices that are deemed restrictive by their very nature insofar as they run counter to the objective of market integration are well identified. They comprise, in essence, conduct aimed at giving absolute territorial protection and restricting exports within the EU.

The analysis shows, on the other hand, that there are still some open questions and uncertainties following decades of enforcement. The alteration of the framework for the evaluation of restrictions is the key practical consequence of the introduction of market integration considerations. Simply put, the assessment of the object of agreements and unilateral practices changes when cross-border is at stake. Instead of focusing on their precise purpose, the evaluation focuses on the means through which the aims sought by the parties are achieved. Cases like *Ping* show that the methodological shift can give rise to confusion in practice. Courts and authorities may conclude, in line with the case law, that a given practice is prima facie unlawful irrespective of its effects. However, they may struggle to justify why they reach a certain outcome. In this sense, much could be gained in terms of legal certainty and clarity if the methodological shift that occurs in practice could be acknowledged and made more explicit.

Second, it is apparent from the case law that territorial restrictions that are in principle unlawful irrespective of their effects can sometimes escape the prohibition and thus fall outside the scope of Articles 101(1) and/or 102 TFEU. This may be due to the fact that the restraints are objectively necessary to attain a pro-competitive aim or because they are incapable of having anticompetitive effects in the economic and legal context of which they are a part. For instance, a practice may not restrict competition – whether by object or effect – where there are 'insurmountable barriers to entry'. As *Generics* confirms, such insurmountable barriers may emerge from the intellectual property system. This could be the case, for instance, where a right is not exhausted in the circumstances of a case or where it is not subject to exhaustion. The Commission's administrative practice, which appears to imply that an agreement may restrict competition by object even in presence of insurmountable barriers, suggests that some uncertainty remains in this regard.

Third, it is notorious that the Commission, since the adoption of Regulation 1/2003, has not prioritised the adoption of decisions declaring that an agreement is either not caught by Article 101(1) TFEU or that it fulfils the conditions set out in Article 101(3) TFEU. The same is true in relation to Article 102 TFEU. As a consequence of the parsimony with which such decisions are adopted, there is precious little guidance on a number of central questions. These include territorial restrictions. It is in principle accepted that some practices that are prima facie unlawful irrespective of their effects can sometimes fulfil the conditions set out in Article 101(3) TFEU. What is more, one can think of circumstances in which they may be justified. At present, however, the administrative practice sheds virtually no light on the question. Some guidance could arguably be beneficial, and not necessarily in conflict with the commitment of the EU competition law system to market integration.

Finally, it would seem that there is potential scope for clarifying the relationship between secondary law instruments and the case law. This is true, in particular, of the interaction between Article 101 TFEU and the VBER. The scope of the notion of restriction by object and that of hardcore restriction within the meaning of the latter are not necessarily identical.[120] However, there is a chance that the two concepts are conflated. The *Character Merchandise*, discussed above, provides a clear example. The Commission claimed, without clear support for its position in the case law, that active sales restraints amount to a restriction by object when imposed in the context of a non-exclusive distribution agreement. The ongoing review of the VBER and, more precisely, the discussion about the instances in which active sales may be restricted, provide an opportunity to clarify these matters and clean up some of the remaining ambiguities.[121]

---

120. Joanna Goyder, *Cet Obscur Objet: Object Restrictions in Vertical Agreements*, 2 Journal of European Competition Law & Practice 327 (2011).

121. *See*, for a discussion of this specific issue, Commission Evaluation of the Vertical Block Exemption Regulation SWD(2020) 172 final. *See*, in particular, p. 125, where the Commission acknowledges that, in the view of the national competition authorities it is not clear from the Guidelines on vertical restraints 'whether exclusive distribution agreements are the only context in which restrictions of active sales are exempted from the hardcore restriction'.

Vertical Restraints and the Digital Revolution: Has the Internet Changed the Rules of the Game in the EU?

Yves Botteman & Alexandra Prohm

1 A BRAVE NEW WORLD?

The Internet has fundamentally changed the way we work, socially interact and shop. A little over a decade ago, when the European Commission (Commission) last reviewed the rules and guidelines on distribution agreements, the approach to e-commerce was centred around the notion that retailers should be given maximum freedom and flexibility to engage in online sales and that suppliers should not impose more limitations on e-commerce than they do in the real world. Since then, the exponential growth of e-commerce has been accompanied by the emergence of successful and powerful intermediaries, including online marketplaces, social networks, online booking platforms, aggregators and price comparison websites.[1] Further, an increasing proportion of suppliers engage in direct selling of their products to consumers through their own online retail shops and compete with their own authorized retailers. Likewise, marketplaces have also entered the retail sector by reselling products themselves. This leads to situations where suppliers and intermediaries are in a dual role and compete with merchants and authorized retailers for the consumer's eyeballs.

As a result, competition at the retail level involves multiple actors and stakeholders with potentially diverging interests and is increasingly complex, namely:

(1) Inter-brand competition among suppliers involves common parameters such as product differentiation, brand recognition and consumer experience, but e-commerce brings them into a new dimension. This requires strategic thinking on how they ought to make use of the online channel to distinguish themselves from their competitors. This will include in particular assessing the extent to which they will make use of marketplaces and social networks, if so, how, and how they can acquire detailed knowledge about consumers, through personal and non-personal data in order to design and develop a unique brand ecosystem.
(2) Large online marketplaces become powerful intermediaries and have their own business model, brand and terms of service, which may not be aligned with those of independent retailers (merchants) and brand suppliers. As antitrust regulators put it,

1. The following documents provide a good overview: European Commission, *Final Report on the E-Commerce Sector Inquiry*, SWD(2017) 154 final, J. Crémer, Y.-A. de Montjoye and H. Schweitzer, *Competition Policy for the Digital Era*, and European Commission, *Support Studies for the Evaluation of the VBER. Final Report*. 2020, e.g., p. 13.

they have become gatekeepers and face potential conflicts of interest as rule-maker, referee and player.[2]

(3) Further, the increased online price transparency and reduced customer search costs led to a significant change of distribution and pricing strategies of both suppliers and retailers over the last ten years. Retailers tend to focus on web traffic to their websites to increase their sales prospects and will often engage in aggressive price campaigns to be noticed and referenced by price aggregators and get to the prominent marketplace rankings. In contrast, suppliers are generally more interested in product positioning, brand image and reputation.

(4) Suppliers also increasingly compete with their (authorized) retailers when they engage in direct selling themselves. As the recent *Hugo Boss*[3] cases illustrate, suppliers of branded goods are not always alert to that competitive dimension between themselves and their distribution networks.

This increased complexity in the relationships between the above operators is compounded by the fact that suppliers also need to integrate and reconcile their online strategy with the offline trade in such a way that the two worlds seamlessly talk to each other. For many suppliers, it is becoming increasingly important to generate a coherent and consistent brand ecosystem that fosters a unique consumer experience.

2. At a Conference on Competition and Digitization, Margrethe Vestager's speech *Digital power at the service of humanity* on 29 Nov. 2019 stated: 'And as digital connections become an ever more important way to bring together buyers and sellers in a market, platforms get more power to shape those markets – power that allows them to act almost as regulators.' The speech is available at: https://wayback.archive-it.org/12090/20191130155750/https://ec.europa.eu/commission/commissioners/2014-2019/vestager/announcements/digital-power-service-humanity_en.

3. Danish Competition Council, decisions of 24 Jun. 2020, Case 19/04380 – *Hugo Boss/Kaufmann* and Case 19/03566 – *Hugo Boss/Ginsborg*.

2 COMPETITION POLICY IN THE DIGITAL ERA: EVALUATION (AND REFORM?) OF THE VBER

It is against this background and the rising importance of e-commerce in our daily lives that the Commission embarked on a review of the Vertical Block Exemption Regulation[4] (VBER) and the Vertical Guidelines[5] (VGL) in October 2018. Unsurprisingly, the stakeholders' contributions to the Commission's evaluation of the VBER and VGL focused on online restraints.[6] Both the VBER and the VGL constitute an important toolkit for brand suppliers and distribution companies active in the European Union (EU) when self-assessing whether their commercial practices employed in vertical relationships are in line with EU competition law. This said, the current framework dates back to 2010. As illustrated above, the explosive boom in e-commerce dramatically changed the commercial and competitive landscape with the emergence of powerful online marketplaces and third-party intermediaries. These changes have already and will continue to affect commercial relations in the years to come. Updating the VBER and the VGL is thus needed to ensure that the EU framework is fit for e-commerce (without neglecting the parallel needs to incorporate recent EU court rulings, foster coherent application of EU competition law in the context of a decentralized enforcement of EU competition law and clarify identified grey areas).

4. Commission Regulation (EU) No 330/2010 of 20 Apr. 2010 on the application of Article 101(3) of the Treaty on the Functioning of the European Union to categories of vertical agreements and concerted practices.

5. Guidelines on vertical restraints, 2010/C 130/01.

6. For an overview of the contributions to the Commission's consultation, *see What are the hot topics for the future of distribution in the European Union?*, available at: https://www.jdsupra.com/legalnews/what-are-the-hot-topics-for-the-future-12998/.

This contribution is structured into two parts. In the first part (*see* section 3 below), we discuss succinctly how courts and competition authorities at EU and Member State level have dealt with attempts by brand suppliers to restrict the ability of retailers to engage in Internet sales. Specifically, this part looks at the various bans that suppliers imposed on retailers in order to reduce the impact of e-commerce on their offline operations and whether the case law that resulted from those restraints provides sufficient guidance to suppliers. In the second part (*see* section 4 below), we take a closer look at one specific price restraint, namely resale price maintenance (RPM). In that second part, we first provide a concise overview of the existing legal rules applicable to RPM in the EU (*see* section 4.1 below), before illustrating via a *tour d'horizon* that RPM is increasingly in the spotlight of (mostly) national competition authorities (NCAs) but also the Commission (*see* section 4.2 below). In the context of a case study taken from real life, we will highlight the problems companies are facing when self-assessing their pricing practices in respects of the VBER and the VGL (*see* section 5.1 below). To conclude (*see* section 5.2 below), we will – advocating for a less rigid and more pragmatic or effects-based approach with respect to certain forms of RPM – present ideas on how to accommodate the existing legal frameworks to the realities of online markets, thereby providing a proposed answer to the *Quo Vadis?*

3 ENFORCEMENT AGAINST ONLINE 'BANS': COURTS AND NCAs BRING CLARITY AT EU AND MEMBER STATES LEVEL, YET GREY AREAS PERSIST

Recent case law is proof of the abundance of potential conflicts between the above actors in e-commerce. Price and non-price related restraints imposed by suppliers, often with the goal to reassert control and bring some sort of discipline into the online space, have been under scrutiny from competition authorities and courts at EU and Member State level.

With regard to non-price online restraints,[7] the enforcement to date has focused on various types of suppliers' induced Internet bans: (i) online sales bans (e.g., *Ping*,[8] *Stihl*,[9] *Bikeurope*[10] and *Guess*[11]) that prevent retailers from engaging in online sales, (ii) online platform bans (e.g., *Coty*,[12] *Stihl*[13] and *Caudalie*[14]) that limit the ability of retailers to work with marketplaces to resell their products, (iii) price comparison tool bans (e.g., *Asics*[15]) that prevent retailers from using price

7. For a detailed discussion on non-price restraints, *see* Botteman & Barrio, *From Pierre Fabre to Coty and Beyond: How Far Can Suppliers Ban Online Sales?*, Journal of European Competition Law & Practice, Volume 10, Issue 9, November 2019, pp. 519-531.

8. UK's Competition and Markets Authority (CMA), decision of 4 Aug. 2017, Case 50230 – *Ping*. This decision has been challenged at the Competition Appeal Tribunal (CAT), decision of 7 Sep. 2018, Case 1279/1/12/17. The CAT dismissed the appeal, but reduced Ping's fine. In its decision of 21 Jan. 2020, Case C3/2018/2863, the Court of Appeal upheld the decisions from the CMA and the CAT in its decision of 21 Jan. 2020, Case C3/2018/2863.

9. French Competition Authority, decision of 24 Oct. 2018, Case 18-D-23 – *Stihl*. This decision of the French Competition Authority has been largely confirmed by the Paris Court of Appeal in its decision of 17 Oct. 2019, Case RG 18/24456. For a discussion on the case, *see* Maillard, Botteman & Keres, *French Competition Authority Revisits Platform Ban in a Post-Coty World*, Kluwer Competition Law Blog, http://competitionlawblog.kluwercompetitionlaw.com/2018/11/13/french-competition-authority-revisits-platform-ban-in-a-post-coty-world/.

10. French Competition Authority, decision of 1 Jul. 2019, Case 19-D-14.

11. European Commission, decision of 17 Dec. 2018, Case AT.40428 – *Guess*.

12. European Court of Justice, judgment of 6 Dec. 2017, Case C-230/16 – *Coty Germany GmbH v. Parfümerie Akzente GmbH*.

13. Paris Court of Appeal, decision of 17 Oct. 2019, Case RG 18/24456. French Competition Authority, decision of 24 Oct. 2018, Case 18-D-23 – *Stihl*.

14. Paris Court of Appeal, decision of 13 Jul. 2018, Case 17/20787 – *Caudalie*.

15. German Federal Court of Justice, judgment of 12 Dec. 2017, Case KVZ 41/17 – *Asics*.

comparison websites, (iv) online advertising and keyword search bans (e.g., *Guess*[16]) that seek to limit the ability of retailers to make use of the brand(s) and associated key terms on search engines, and (v) cross-border sales bans (e.g., *Pioneer*[17] and *Guess*[18]) that limit the consumer's ability to engage in e-commerce with retailers operating outside of their country of residence.

In reaching their conclusion whether such bans constituted naked violations (under the *by object*[19] standard) of EU and national competition rules, authorities and courts have invariably relied on the basic notion that retailers should not be subject to egregious limitations on their ability to engage in online selling. Put differently, the focus of the antitrust assessment has been whether the ban effectively prevents retailers from accessing and being visible to consumers on the Internet. Apart from the European Court of Justice (ECJ) ruling in *Coty*[20] that concluded that a marketplace ban did not amount to a limitation on retailers' ability to engage in online sales, all the other bans were considered to impose undue limitations on the retailers' freedom to operate.

16. European Commission, decision of 17 Dec. 2018, Case AT.40428 – *Guess*. For a discussion of the case, *see* Botteman, *Guess Where Enforcement Stands Post E-Commerce Sector Inquiry?*, Kluwer Competition Law Blog, http://competitionlawblog.kluwercompetitionlaw.com/2019/02/14/guess-where-enforcement-stands-post-e-commerce-sector-inquiry/.

17. European Commission, decision of 24 Jul. 2018, Case AT.40182 – *Pioneer*.

18. European Commission, decision of 17 Dec. 2018, Case AT.40428 – *Guess*.

19. A restriction by object is an agreement or collusive behaviour that, by its very nature and based on experience, can be regarded as being highly distortive of competition and harmful to consumers without it being necessary to look into its actual anticompetitive effects.

20. European Court of Justice, judgment of 6 Dec. 2017, Case C-230/16 – *Coty Germany GmbH v. Parfümerie Akzente GmbH*. *See* Botteman & Barrio, *The Coty Exception: A Luxury for a Selected Few?*, Kluwer Competition Law Blog, http://competitionlawblog.kluwercompetitionlaw.com/2017/12/15/coty-exception-luxury-selected/.

This being said, those cases dealt with outright online bans. In many situations, though, suppliers do not impose bans but rather impose strict conditions on the use of online tools such as online search and price comparison websites. In the context of selective distribution, such restraints will be assessed through the lens of the *Metro*[21] criteria and the principle of equivalence (as set forth in the VGL). Ultimately, though, this question will revolve around whether the practice is adequate and proportionate in view of the objectives pursued by the supplier. We suspect that, in the future, disputes will revolve around the extent to which the supplier's strict conditions on the use of the e-commerce channel by retailers will be considered excessive in view of the brand, the product and the supplier's overall approach to the Internet. To date, the EU and national case law as well as the VBER and its accompanying guidelines (VGL) have provided limited guidance in this increasingly grey(ish) zone. This being said, while outright 'bans' may well fall in the *by object* category because such limitations invariably lead to a significant impediment on the ability of retailers to engage in online sales, it is submitted that other e-commerce limitations that fall short of a ban ought to be assessed under an effects-based framework.

4 RPM AND THE ONLINE SPACE: A CHANGE IN PARADIGM?

Turning to price limitations, RPM is by far the most common restriction of competition in e-commerce, making effective enforcement of competition law in this area particularly

21. European Court of Justice, judgment of 25 Oct. 1977, Case 26/76 – *Metro SB-Großmärkte GmbH & CO. KG v. Commission.*

significant.[22] As we will discuss further below, the evaluation[23] and the likely reform of the VBER and VGL offer an opportunity to reflect and reassess the theories of harm and the enforcement approach towards RPM. This is particularly needed in the context of e-commerce overtaking high street shopping.

4.1 Recap on the EU Legal Framework Governing RPM

RPM refers to agreements or concerted practices between a supplier and a reseller with the object of directly or indirectly establishing a fixed or minimum price[24] or price level to be observed by the dealer when reselling a product/service to his customers.[25] As a general rule, RPM will be considered to

22. *Support Studies for the Evaluation of the VBER. Final Report*, 2020, p. 40. With 222 reported cases, price restrictions are clearly the vertical restraints most commonly investigated by NCAs in the Member States. About 210 of these cases relate to RPM, eleven cases relate to recommended resale prices and four cases to the imposition of maximum resale prices.

23. The purpose of the evaluation is to verify whether the VBER is still 'effective, efficient, relevant, in line with other EU legislation and adds value'. The process started with an evaluation phase in late 2018 during which evidence on the functioning of the VBER together with the accompanying VGL was gathered. Almost twenty-five organizations provided the Commission with feedback. Until end of May 2019, the public could submit contributions to a public consultation. The Commission plans to publish the results of that consultation in the form of a Staff Working document in the second quarter of 2020. Further details are available at https://ec.europa.eu/info/law/better-regulation/have-your-say/initiatives/1936-Evaluation-of-the-Vertical-Block-Exemption-Regulation. Most recently, the Commission has published *Support Studies for the Evaluation of the Vertical Block Exemption Regulation*.

24. Please note that the EU concept of RPM also englobes the frequently used minimum advertised prices (MAP) obligations. MAPs are set by the manufacturer of goods or services and effectively prevent retailers from advertising or promoting the products or services below MAP.

25. *See*, e.g., *Support Studies for the Evaluation of the VBER. Final Report*. 2020, p. 84.

constitute a hardcore restriction within the meaning of Article 4(1) lit. a) VBER. As such, RPM is considered illegal *by object*. This rather strict stance is considered to be justified, among others, because this form of vertical price fixing is apt to prevent both retail and wholesale price competition.[26]

Back in 2010, the Commission nonetheless recognized in the VGL that RPM may exceptionally have pro-competitive effects and crafted relatively narrow and concise exceptions.[27] The Commission provides three examples where RPM could be exempted under Article 101(3) TFEU if a case-by-case analysis clearly and convincingly demonstrates that it leads to efficiencies (at least some of which are passed on to consumers). First, RPM might be helpful where a manufacturer introduces a new product as it can help to induce distributors to better take into account the manufacturer's interest to promote the product during the introductory period of expanding demand.[28] Second, RPM may be necessary to organize in a franchise system or similar distribution system applying a uniform distribution format for a coordinated short-term low price campaign (two to six weeks in most cases). Third, the extra margin provided by RPM may allow retailers to provide (additional) presales services, in particular, in case of experience or complex products.[29]

---

26. Further considerations are provided in the VGL, para. 224.

27. VGL, para. 225. *See also* Botteman, *(Minimum) Resale Price Maintenance under the New Guidelines: A Critique and a Suggestion*, Competition Policy International, January 2010, https://www.competitionpolicyinternational.com/minimum-resale-price-maintenance-under-the-new-guidelines-a-critique-and-a-suggestion/.

28. In such a case, RPM may provide the distributors with the means to increase sales efforts. Further, and in case that the distributors in this market are under competitive pressure, it may induce them to expand overall demand for the product and make the launch of the product a success.

29. The Commission highlights that if enough customers take advantage of such services to decide on a product but ultimately purchase it at a lower price with retailers that do

4.2 The State of RPM Enforcement to Date

Although, according to the VBER and the VGL, RPM constitutes a hardcore restriction, it has not been – until fairly recently – an enforcement priority of the Commission.[30] For the most part, over the years, NCAs took over the lead role in vigorously prosecuting RPM.

Without being exhaustive and by way of illustration, the German Federal Cartel Office[31] fined undertakings from the food retail sector,[32] Lego,[33] fashion[34] and the bicycle wholesaler ZEG.[35] The Austrian Federal Competition Authority fined undertakings from the food retail sector a total of EUR 60 million[36] and a manufacturer of electronic devices.[37] Recently, the French Competition Authority fined Apple and two

not provide such services (and hence do not incur these costs), service retailers may reduce or eliminate these services that enhance the demand for the supplier's product. The Commission recognizes that RPM may help to prevent such free riding at the distribution level.

30. The last Commission decision on RPM dates back to 2003 in *Yamaha*. European Commission, decision of 16 Jul. 2003, Case COMP 37/975 – *Yamaha*.

31. The German Federal Cartel Office published a guidance paper on RPM with focus on the food and retail sector (in German only), available at: https://www.bundeskartellamt.de/SharedDocs/Publikation/DE/Diskussions_Hintergrundpapier/Hinweispapier%20Preisbindung%20im%20Lebensmitteleinzelhandel.pdf;jsessionid=F5E14788C508BD8980DB3A7446198BC6.1_cid371?__blob=publicationFile&v=8.

32. German Federal Cartel Office, Case B10-20/15 – *Beer*; Case B10-040/14 – *Sweets*, Case B10-041/14 – *Ritter Chocolate*, Case B10-50/14 – *Coffee*.

33. German Federal Cartel Office, press release of 12 Jan. 2016 – *Lego*.

34. German Federal Cartel Office, Case B2-62/16 – *Wellenstein*.

35. German Federal Cartel Office, Case B11-28/16 – *ZEG*.

36. Higher Regional Court of Vienna, judgment of 3 Mar. 2016, Case 26 Kt 2/16 – *Rauch*, judgment of 30 Jun. 2016, Case 29 Kt 10/16 – *INTERSPAR and others*, judgment of 3.3.2015, Case 25 Kt 76/14 – *Vösslauer*.

37. Higher Regional Court of Vienna, judgment of 14 Nov. 2016, Case 25 Kt 6/16 – *DeLonghi-Kenwood*, judgment of 9 Sep. 2015, Case 24 Kt 35/15 – *Samsung*. The Austrian Federal Competition Authority published a guidance paper on vertical price

other big tech companies a total of EUR 1.1 billion for anticompetitive practices including resale price fixing.[38] Not long ago, the UK Competition and Markets Authority imposed fines for agreements in the light fitting sector,[39] the commercial catering equipment [40] and the bathroom-fitting sector.[41] Other national competition authorities have also started to pursue vertical restraints more actively. Examples include the Dutch[42] and the Belgian Competition Authorities.[43]

The Commission apparently changed its focus in the course of the e-commerce sector inquiry where it found that online price limitations were widespread.[44] Since then, the Commission reasserted its interest in the topic. In particular,

fixing, available at: https://www.bwb.gv.at/fileadmin/user_upload/PDFs/BWB-Leitfaden%20-%20Standpunkt%20zu%20vertikalen%20Preisbindungen.pdf.

38. French Competition Authority, decision of 16 Mar. 2020, Case 20-D-04 – *Apple, Tech Data and Ingram Micro* (the case is under appeal). On 20 Dec. 2018, the authority fined several producers and wholesale distributors of liquid fertilizers for RPM, Case 18-D-26.

39. UK's Competition and Markets Authority, decision of 3 May 2017, Case 50343 – *Light fitting sector.*

40. UK's Competition and Markets Authority, decision of 24 May 2016, Case CE/9856-14 – *Commercial catering equipment sector.*

41. UK's Competition and Markets Authority, decision of 10 May 2016, Case CE/9857-14 – *Bathroom-fitting sector.*

42. In the context of the Fifteenth Annual Conference of the GCLC, *Vertical Restraints in the Digital Economy: VBER Reform and the Future of Distribution*, the head of the Dutch Competition Authority said that RPM has risen in the authority's priority list. The Dutch Competition Authority investigated price-fixing agreements between consumer goods manufacturers and retailers, *see* its press release of 27 Dec. 2018.

43. Most recently, the Belgian Competition Authority adopted a settlement decision in a case concerning a practice of RPM, decision of 24 Jan. 2019, Case 19-IO-03-AUD, decision of 22 Mar. 2017, Case 17-IO-07-AUD – *Algist Bruggeman*, decision of 22 Jun. 2015, Case 15-IO-19-AUD.

44. European Commission, *Final Report on the E-Commerce Sector Inquiry*, SWD(2017) 154 final.

in 2018, the Commission fined Asus,[45] Denon & Marantz,[46] Philips[47] and Pioneer[48] for RPM and cross sales restrictions with approximately EUR 111 million. These fines appear somewhat high considering the short timeframe of the infringements (two to three years maximum) and clearly sent a strong signal to the market. A novelty here was that certain suppliers used price-monitoring software to ensure effective compliance with its RPM. Pioneer, for instance, used such a tool to monitor the online prices of its dealers and was thus able to intervene quickly when sales prices were considered too low. The price-monitoring software allowed Pioneer to find out which dealer was responsible for the price reduction and was able to approach him directly with a view to raising the resale price. In doing so, it prevented price erosion in the online sphere. Finally, in 2019, the Commission fined Guess[49] for restrictions on cross-border sales and RPM.

One key lesson from the above overview is that, in most cases, investigated companies were under pressure to settle their RPM cases before the Commission and the NCAs. Authorities sit on the VBER and enjoy a very comfortable prosecutorial position, leaving suppliers with virtually no option but to quickly wave the white flag, admit their sin and settle against a lower penalty. As most cases were settled, antitrust enforcers did not have to explain and justify in detail in their decisions why and in what way the RPM conduct in

45. European Commission, decision of 24 Jul. 2018, Case AT.40465 – *Asus*.

46. European Commission, decision of 24 Jul. 2018, Case AT.40469 – *Denon & Marantz*.

47. European Commission, decision of 24 Jul. 2018, Case AT.40181 – *Philips*.

48. European Commission, decision of 24 Jul. 2018, Case AT.40182 – *Pioneer*.

49. European Commission, decision of 17 Dec. 2018, Case AT.40428 – *Guess*. Although the fine of EUR 40 million was not only imposed for vertical price fixing, it did play an important role. A greater focus, however, was placed on the identified obstacles to cross-border trade and online trade.

question invariably resulted in significant consumer harm with no sufficient cognizable efficiencies to outweigh the alleged harm. This means that in stark contrast to the decisions on online bans discussed above - a significant number of which were ultimately decided by courts -, the anticompetitive effects of RPM have not been subject to in-depth discussion and judicial review. This is significant as the debate around RPM usually builds on the notion that there is ample empirical evidence that RPM is inevitably leading to higher prices, which cannot be justified or outweighed by countervailing pro-consumer considerations, such as appropriate product positioning, product availability or investment in high quality products and pre- and after-sale services.

5 CALL FOR A NEW ENFORCEMENT PARADIGM?

This leads us to a rather inconvenient truth: For decades, RPM has been considered an EU competition law infringement *by object*, which spares the enforcing authority from the duty to prove any harmful effect. The overwhelming trend to settle RPM cases results in cursory analyses of why RPM is problematic in a given case.[50] Worse, the harmful effects of RPM have largely remained untested in EU and national courts. Economic efficiencies and pro-consumer justifications have virtually no place as potential defences in this area of antitrust enforcement.

The current framework set forth in the VBER and the VGL is concerning for at least two reasons. From a theoretical

50. Even in the absence of settlements, authorities provided little insights into the alleged harmful effects on competition. In the recent *Apple* case, the French Competition Authority did not engage in a detailed analysis of the impact the conduct had on consumers.

standpoint, *by object* violations are considered to be invariably harmful, irrespective of the market position of the undertakings involved. There is no *de minimis* threshold under which a practice falling within the *by object* category may be considered as minor and hence withstand scrutiny.[51] This said, there is no doubt that RPM is capable of generating harmful effects when: (a) the supplier enjoys significant market power (i.e., there is a lack of inter-brand competition) or (b) the practice is engaged in simultaneously by a number of competing suppliers in a tight oligopoly or induced by powerful resellers. Yet, outside those scenarios (captured at paragraph 224 of the VGL), the anticompetitive effects of RPM are less clear and, in our view, should be empirically demonstrated in every given case. This should not be coming as a surprise as vertical integration is usually associated with efficiency gains (e.g., eliminating the double marginalization) and solving free-riding and commitment problems. As a result, one can already *see* the *by object* standard colliding with RPM as a vertical restraint.

From a compliance perspective, suppliers are being told and advised that RPM is a hardcore restriction and hence to be avoided at all cost. At the same time, in a rather cursory and vague way, the VGL opens a very narrow path for justifying certain RPM practices. Conceptually, it is difficult to erect a conduct as a *by object* one (i.e., assigned to the most serious violations of EU competition law), and at the same time say that – in a narrow set of circumstances – RPM might be beneficial to resolve a free-riding and commitment problem, and withstand a detailed Article 101(3) TFEU analysis. As discussed below, few companies, if any, have tried to walk

51. European Court of Justice, judgment of 13 Dec. 2012, Case C-226/11 – *Expedia v. Autorité de la Concurrence & Others*.

such a thin line and when they did, they took an abundance of precautions in order to green-light such a practice.

Finally, the malaise is aggravated by the ECJ rulings in two horizontal cases, *Groupement des Cartes Bancaires*,[52] and more recently, *Budapest Bank*,[53] by which the court sought to narrow down the scope of *by object* infringements to practices on which an ample body of empirical evidence and experience as to their harmful effects on competition exists. How can we reconcile that case law that dealt with horizontal price fixing with the continued harsh stance against RPM, which, as indicated above, is a vertical conduct whose effects are unclear in the absence of market power and/or capable of generating efficiencies?

5.1 RPM and E-Commerce: A Case Study

As discussed above, e-commerce has fundamentally complexified the chain of supply. Suppliers, making widespread use of selective distribution, have attempted to align and reconcile the interests of online merchants. However, in a number of situations, this has proven to be particularly challenging.

Consider the following example, taken from recent experience. A supplier of high-end consumer goods is in the process of launching a new product. The product development has required significant upfront investments in R&D and

52. European Court of Justice, judgment of 11 Sep. 2014, Case C-67/13 P – *Groupement des Cartes Bancaires v. European Commission*.

53. European Court of Justice, judgment of 2 Apr. 2020, Case C-228/18 – *Budapest Bank and others*. For a discussion of the case, *see* Botteman & Keres, *AG Bobek's Opinion in Budapest Bank: On Object vs. Effect, Fish and Lilies*, Kluwer Competition Law Blog, http://competitionlawblog.kluwercompetitionlaw.com/2019/10/04/ag-bobeks-opinion-in-budapest-bank-on-object-vs-effect-fish-and-lilies/.

engineering, and the whole process has taken several years. Prior to effective launch and mass production, the supplier showcases prototypes and organizes a PR campaign. However, past experience with product launches proved disastrous. In particular, as soon as the new product was presented to the public, influent e-retailers engaged in aggressive price campaigns, offering the new product at heavily discounted retail prices (well below the suggested launch price). Such practice is predominantly driven by their eagerness to gain visibility and to draw traffic to their websites. Often, this was done while the e-retailer had no inventory and had not placed a single order for the new product. The resulting effect of such early price depression was that wholesalers and other retailers were less enthusiastic about investing in marketing launch efforts and even purchasing the product at the original wholesale price. As a result, the product launch generated far lower initial orders from wholesalers and retailers, causing the product not to be widely available to early adopters, which in turn negatively affected product take-up. Ultimately, sales volumes were significantly under the expected budget and the supplier gradually reduced production runs. The return on the investment was well below the expectations.

In order to avoid a similar outcome this time around, the supplier considered relying on the narrow exception provided for in paragraph 225 of the VGL, which states that 'where a manufacturer introduces a new product, RPM may be helpful during the introductory period of expanding demand to induce distributors to better take into account the manufacturer's interest to promote the product'. However, the exception goes on to say that such recourse to RPM is preconditioned on the assumption that 'it is not practical for the supplier to impose on all [resellers] by contract effective promotion requirements'. This condition is understood to mean that

RPM can only be a solution of last resort, where it appears that other alternative ways to seek and obtain alignment and engagement from all resellers would be ineffective or difficult to achieve.

In the case at hand, the supplier faced a number of practical hurdles making it difficult to impose promotional requirements on all resellers. Among others, its selective distribution system was in its infancy – the marketing efforts imposed on online resellers were rather light – and the channel was not watertight (which is almost impossible to achieve in practice).

Before deciding to impose RPM on its resellers during the launch phase of the product, there was significant uncertainty as to what constituted a 'new' product as well as to what would be a reasonable 'introductory period'. Given the stakes involved but also the significant risks of getting it wrong and be subject to prosecution by one or more antitrust authorities, the supplier took a very conservative approach to novelty and duration of the launch phase, in that case three months. Similarly, the supplier provided a clear end date to its RPM to ensure that resellers understood that this obligation would only apply for a quarter.

The real-life example above illustrates that the VGL conditions for new product launch RPM are not only quite vague and onerous but create significant uncertainty. In particular, the supplier has to overcome potential objections that it should have invested adequate time and resources in the design and implementation of a watertight and sophisticated distribution model that would have made RPM unnecessary. In that respect, a common objection asserts that selective distribution could effectively solve the free-riding problem identified above. Further, a fair reading of the exception of paragraph 225 strongly suggests that the supplier must be able to show that: (i) he actually considered several ways to induce online resellers – including dual pricing which in itself is not without antitrust risks,[54] or contractually agreed marketing budgets – to promote and position the product in a manner that meets the supplier's objectives and (ii) that those alternative ways proved impractical or ineffective. Finally, as illustrated above, it is unclear how new is a new product (e.g., does it have to be revolutionary or substantially different from prior generations?) and what is the acceptable duration of an introductory period (which may vary depending on the product and the distribution channel).

A similar critique could be made of the other exceptions provided for in paragraph 225, namely the short-term low price campaign in a franchise or similar system and the exception relating to experience or complex goods. In conclusion, the VGL exceptions to RPM are too vague and onerous to be of any practical use by the overwhelming majority of suppliers. Put another way, faced with a high risk of being prosecuted under the *by object* standard, suppliers would need a more articulate and structured safe harbour for RPM.

5.2 Ways to Adapt the VBER

The scope and purpose of this contribution is not to enter into a detailed economic debate to challenge the proclaimed harmful effects commonly associated with RPM. Rather, our modest objective is to highlight that the current enforcement framework lacks sufficient economic and empirical basis and that it should be adapted to embrace the new world that

54. *See* the commitments offered by Lego in France: French Competition Authority, press release of 30 Jul. 2020.

e-commerce has created. In short, maintaining the *status quo* does not seem to be an option.

In this regard, several routes for reform are on the table, two of which are probably worth exploring. A first approach would consist of taking stock of the ECJ case law on *by object* versus *by effect* infringements (not only *Cartes Bancaires* and *Budapest Bank* but also *Intel*[55] on exclusionary rebates). Under such an approach, a supplier should be able – as long as he lacks market power and operates in a sufficiently contestable inter-brand market – to articulate a plausible (efficiency) justification in support of RPM, which in turn would shift the analysis from a *by object* to a *by effect* framework. In sum, the RPM *by object* box would be narrowed down to the most egregious situations for which there are enough supporting economic theory and empirical evidence.

Another solution would be to broaden and clarify the exceptions for RPM in order to make them more practical and accessible to suppliers. This may involve setting a safe harbour with relevant metrics, including market share thresholds, market concentration ratios and product scope or life cycle considerations (i.e., the more recent the product, the more the supplier will seek to protect the initial wholesale and retail price points).

55. European Court of Justice, judgment of 6 Sep. 2017, Case C-413/14 P – *Intel*.

Assessment of MFNs in the Digital World: The Case for a More Effects-Based Approach

*Avantika Chowdhury**

This chapter discusses the approach towards assessment of most favoured nation (MFN) clauses in Europe from an economic perspective. Given the growth of digital platforms and e-commerce more broadly, specific discussion on MFNs in the new VBER will be critical for developing a consistent approach across Europe. In this context, this chapter posits that it is essential that MFN clauses are assessed using an effects-based approach. We also discuss the economic analysis of free riding and posit that such analysis needs to be undertaken as part of the assessment of competitive effects and not reserved for an efficiency defence.

1 INTRODUCTION

The rise of e-commerce and online services in the last decade and the accompanying changes in consumer behaviour, business models and practices have been documented widely.

* The views expressed in this chapter are the author's alone and do not represent the views of any other person or company.

There appears to be a broad consensus that revisions to the Vertical Block Exemption Regulation (VBER) and/or the accompanying Vertical Guidelines are needed to ensure that they remain relevant and effective in this new environment.[1] On the one hand, the digital environment has reduced search costs for consumers and increased the scope for suppliers to reach larger and more varied audiences and/or new entrants to challenge existing business models. This has increased the scope for more competition, and consequently, also the concerns around any practice that might hinder this competition (such as limiting the number or type of online retailers of a product). At the same time, the digital environment strengthens potential pro-competitive justifications of many vertical agreements, for example, because of the increased scope for free riding by consumers. This has raised questions around how the assessment of vertical agreements should account for and balance these two opposing effects, and whether these effects warrant a significant change in the VBER.

In this chapter, we discuss these questions in the context of MFN clauses. As found by the support study for the evaluation of the VBER published in 2020, there has been a large-scale growth in the use of MFNs across sectors. We have also witnessed a number of investigations in the online hotel

1. *See*, e.g., responses to the Commission's consultation by industry participants and practitioners, views from national competition authorities and findings of the survey conducted in the support study published by the Commission in May 2020 (*see* European Commission, *Review of the Vertical Block Exemption Regulation*, sections 2-5, https://ec.europa.eu/competition/consultations/2018_vber/index_en.html), and summary in European Commission, *Commission Staff Working Document: Evaluation of the Vertical Block Exemption Regulation* (8 September 2020), https://ec.europa.eu/competition/consultations/2018_vber/staff_working_document.pdf.

booking sector by different national competition authorities, which did not always adopt consistent approaches and decisions. In this context, specific discussion on MFNs in the new VBER will be critical for developing a consistent approach across Europe. Below, we discuss, from an economic perspective, why it is critical that MFN clauses benefit from the block exemption (i.e., are not considered 'hardcore') and importantly, are assessed using a proper effects-based approach. We also discuss the economic analysis of free riding and posit that such analysis needs to be undertaken as part of the assessment of competitive effects and not reserved for an efficiency defence.[2,3]

2 LEARNINGS FROM PAST CASES AND EX POST ASSESSMENTS

A good starting point for considering the future of MFNs is to look at the past. There have been a number of investigations into MFNs in the last decade, mostly at the national level. Some notable ones include investigations into the supply of e-books, online hotel booking services, footwear, motor insurance, and home insurance. While some of these ended with infringement decisions, many culminated in commitments.

2. This is consistent with recent commentary from legal practitioners, including recent case law such as *Budapest Bank* and *Generics (UK)*. Case C-307/18, *Generics (UK) Ltd and others v. Competition and Markets Authority*; Case C-228/18, *Gazdasági Versenyhivatal v. Budapest Bank Nyrt. and Others*. For a detailed legal analysis of this point, *see* P. Ibáñez Colomo, *Vertical Restraints after Generics and Budapest Bank* (31 August 2020), https://papers.ssrn.com/sol3/papers.cfm?abstract_id=3683938.

3. Much of the discussion in this chapter, particularly with regard to free riding, is relevant also to other vertical agreements, such as selective distribution systems.

Of these, it was the series of investigations into MFN clauses between hotels and online travel agent (OTA) platforms that brought MFNs into the limelight.[4] These clauses meant that a room of a specific hotel advertised on a specific OTA need to be offered at a price that is no higher than the price of the same room at other distribution channels. In other words, the OTA with the MFN clause could offer the room to consumers at the 'best' price. The MFN could cover all distribution channels, i.e., all other OTAs and the hotel's own website, in which case it would be referred to as a 'wide MFN'. Alternatively, it could cover the hotel's website only, and no other OTAs. This would be referred to as a 'narrow MFN' (here, the hotel could offer a lower price through another OTA, but not on its own website). The key concern was that these MFN clauses offer the OTA in question protection from competition from other channels and therefore reduce intra-brand competition, which may, in turn, lead OTAs to increase the commissions they charge to the hotel.

Despite investigations by more than ten national competition authorities, these cases provided limited clarity around the assessment of MFN clauses. For example, the German competition authority concluded that the wide MFNs as well as the narrow MFNs were anticompetitive. Some authorities accepted commitments from platforms, such as Expedia and Booking.com, to remove the wide MFNs, but allowed narrow MFNs to be used. Yet some others, like the UK competition authority, framed their investigation as one into resale price maintenance and not MFNs, while in some countries (such as

4. The first of these investigations was led by the Bundeskartellamt (BKA), which was followed by multiple other national competition authorities (including Austria, France, Hungary, Italy, Switzerland and Sweden).

France and Italy), all MFNs were banned by an amendment of the law.[5]

This variation across countries, along with the outcome of subsequent appeals, underlines the current lack of clarity and the need for guidance from the Commission. For example, the German decision to ban narrow MFNs was reversed in 2019 by the Düsseldorf Higher Regional Court.[6] The Court disagreed with the competition authority and found that the narrow MFNs were permissible. The Court noted that, without the narrow MFN clauses, hotels could use the OTA's service to advertise themselves, but subsequently attract consumers to book directly on their own websites through lower prices, which may undermine the OTA business model.[7]

There have also been a number of *ex post* assessments of MFN cases, notably the above hotel booking cases and the motor insurance investigation in the UK. Most of these *ex post* assessments involved empirical analyses of the ban on wide (and in some cases, narrow) MFNs. The analyses used surveys among hotels as well as sophisticated quantitative analysis of market data on prices of hotels at various channels.

5. The commitments from Expedia and Booking.com were to remove all wide MFNs across Europe and to reduce the scope of narrow MFNs to only the hotel's price on its online direct sales channel. This meant that following the commitments, hotels could set prices freely on other OTAs and on offline channels (such as telephones, walk-ins) and within their loyalty programmes. The Europe-wide removal of wide MFNs followed Booking.com's commitments to the French, Italian and Swedish competition authorities in 2015. Subsequently, narrow MFNs were also banned in four specific countries (Austria, Belgium, France and Italy) through amendments to national laws.
6. Düsseldorf Higher Regional Court, Decision of 4 June 2019, Case No. VI (Kart) 2/16 (V).
7. This judgment is in the process of being appealed by the BKA at the time of writing this chapter.

While the level of clarity provided by these studies is arguable, they have significantly contributed to the debate around the economic analysis of the effects of MFN clauses. For example, the most recent analysis examines the prohibition of narrow MFNs in three countries (Austria, Belgium, and Italy) using econometric models of hotel prices over time.[8] In essence, this analysis compares prices in these three countries relative to other (benchmark) countries where narrow MFNs continue to be used, while accounting for differences in other factors across countries. The study concludes that the ban on narrow MFNs was followed by significant decreases in hotel prices, indicating the anticompetitive effect of narrow MFNs.

While the approach adopted in this study is sophisticated, the methodology and the results are not without important drawbacks and limitations, and these, at the very least, call into question the findings of the study.[9] Similarly, an earlier *ex post* study of the ban on wide MFNs in the same sector has not produced clear convincing findings.[10] Some would argue that

---

8. European Commission, *Support Studies for the Evaluation of the VBER*, Final Report (May 2020), https://ec.europa.eu/competition/publications/reports/kd0420219enn.pdf.

9. For example, one of the models uses highly aggregated price indices for a set of countries, which can be influenced by a range of factors unconnected to MFNs. For instance, in some countries that are used as benchmarks in the model, the data shows an (unexplained) increase in this price index over time, while such an increase is not seen in the three countries (Austria, Belgium and Italy) where narrow MFNs were banned. This drives part of the finding that a ban on narrow MFNs in Austria, Belgium and Italy reduced prices relative to the benchmark countries without this ban. However, this upward trend was present only in some of the benchmark countries and could have been driven by reasons unrelated to MFNs. Similarly, there are questions around the sample size and representativeness of the part of the empirical analysis (the model which utilises granular, hotel-level prices, covers only ninety-five hotels across twenty-eight European cities).

10. European Commission and the Belgian, Czech, French, German, Hungarian, Irish, Italian, Dutch, Swedish and UK national competition authorities, *Report on the Monitoring Exercise Carried out in the Online Hotel Booking Sector by the EU*

this study showed that wide MFNs did not, in fact, have a harmful effect in the hotel sector; while some others may interpret the results as merely showing that the market was not functioning as it should have after the ban (for instance, due to lack of awareness of hotels regarding the ban), and this is the reason why the study did not find evidence of clear positive effects of the ban of wide MFNs.[11] Notwithstanding, and as we discuss below, these studies do inform, to some extent, the broad approach that is likely to be appropriate for the assessment of MFNs.

3 DO WE NEED A NEW APPROACH?

In the context of the revision of the VBER, one may pose two questions. First, whether MFNs (be it wide or narrow) should benefit from the safe harbours of the VBER, i.e., whether they should continue to fall outside the hardcore list. The second question is whether an effects-based approach is warranted for the assessment of these clauses. In other words, are MFNs anticompetitive by their 'very nature' and should they be assessed using a 'by object' approach,[12] or does one need to use an effects-based approach?

Competition Authorities in 2016 (April 2017), https://ec.europa.eu/competition/ecn/hotel_monitoring_report_en.pdf.

11. For example, the results showed that there was no clear evidence that commission rates had changed between July 2015 and June 2016, and around 90% of hotels saw no difference in the commissions charged by the OTAs. In the survey, more than 80% of hotels that replied said that they did not change their behaviour after the MFN clauses were removed.

12. *See, e.g.*, P. Ibáñez Colomo, *Vertical Restraints after Generics and Budapest Bank* (31 August 2020), discussing the application of the 'by-object' approach with reference to recent case law. *See also* Case C-67/13 P, *Groupement des Cartes Bancaires (CB) v. European Commission*, paras 56-58; Case C-228/18, *Gazdasági Versenyhivatal v. Budapest Bank Nyrt. and Others*, para. 76.

From an economic perspective, both these questions relate to the potential economic effects, positive or negative, of MFN clauses. Specifically, an economic approach would strongly support that MFN clauses should not be considered hardcore restrictions.

Furthermore, we posit that the lessons from recent cases, the wider economic literature and the various *ex post* analyses conducted by competition authorities all, in fact, suggest that the assessment of MFN clauses under Article 101 warrants an effects-based approach.

First, the academic literature shows that the effect of MFNs depends on a range of factors and the combination of these factors critically influences the net impact on end consumers. This literature includes theoretical papers which model MFNs in various settings (e.g., in the context of agency agreements versus wholesale agreements, cases where potential entrants have similar versus different business models, and markets with commission structures based on revenue sharing versus other structures). Overall, the theoretical studies show that the net effect depends on the specific market and commercial setup assumed in the models.[13] Indeed, this increases the importance of empirical testing of the effects of

13. For example, some early work by Corts (1997) include a theoretical model which shows that price-matching policies can lower equilibrium prices if firms are adopting a price-beating approach; K.S. Corts, *On the Competitive Effect of Price-Matching Policies*, International Journal of Industrial Organization, Vol. 15, Issue 3, 283-299 (1997). Johnson (2017) finds in a theoretical model that MFN clauses increase prices when used with an agency model, while noting that in an agency model, MFNs may facilitate higher choice without higher prices under certain contractual settings (e.g., if retailers face market-entry costs and when parties use profit sharing rather than revenue sharing); J.P. Johnson, *The Agency Model and MFN Clauses*, The Review of Economic Studies, Vol. 84, Issue 3, 1151-1185 (2017); also *see* A. Boik and K.S. Corts, *The Effects of Platform MFNs on Competition and Entry*, The Journal of Law and Economics, Vol. 59, 105-134 (2016). Other papers highlight the risk from MFNs, depending on the market concentration both at supplier level and retail level, and

such clauses. In fact, there are many studies that do so, including a large number on the online hotel booking sector, taking advantage of the antitrust enforcement mentioned earlier. In addition, academics have examined MFNs clauses in e-books, consumer electronics and a range of other consumer goods. Similar to the theoretical papers, the empirical studies show that the effects of MFN clauses vary depending on the specific market context.[14]

All the above suggest that analysing the actual or likely effects of MFN clauses in the specific context of a case is important to be able to appropriately assess the risks and benefits and the net effect on consumers.

Second, the *ex post* assessments in the hotel sector discussed above provide broad support for an effects-based approach. Indeed, it is by itself interesting that the 2017 report on the monitoring exercise in EU (assessing the impact of wide MFNs) and the 2020 Support Study (analysing the impact of narrow MFNs) both carried out extensive econometric modelling to assess the impact of the bans imposed. As

---

market coverage of MFNs. *See, e.g.*, Salop and Scott Morton, *Developing an Administrable MFN Enforcement Policy*, Antitrust, Vol. 27, Issue 2, 15-19 (2013); and Edelman and Wright, *Price Coherence and Excessive Intermediation*, The Quarterly Journal of Economics, Vol. 130, Issue 3, 1283-1328 (2015). There are some other recent theoretical models which show pro-competitive effects, for example when suppliers have a higher bargaining power: *see* T. Larrieu, *Most Favoured Nation Clauses on the Online Booking Market*, Working Paper (2019).

14. For example, one study by Chen et al. (2011) on the impact of Best Buy's MFN clauses on consumer electronics found that price decreased after the introduction of the clauses, while another study found that the price impact depends on whether consumers value the services offered in the physical stores. J. Chen and Q. Liu, *The Effect of Most-Favored Customer Clauses on Prices*, The Journal of Industrial Economics, Vol. 59, No. 3, 343-371 (2011); and C. Wu, K. Wang and T. Zhu, *Can Price Matching Defeat Showrooming?* (2015). *See also* the Commission's support study, section 8.2.

discussed above, there are a large number of aspects (technical and non-technical) on which these studies, and their findings, can be (and have been) challenged.

This is consistent with the view that MFN clauses are not anticompetitive by their 'very nature' but rather the effect depends on the specific market context, which lends support for an effects-based analysis.[15]

4 RELEVANT CONSIDERATIONS FOR AN EFFECTS-BASED ANALYSIS

The economic literature and other studies show that a range of factors affect the impact of MFNs on intra- and inter-brand competition and on consumer outcomes. These include, for example, the extent of use of MFNs by market players, such as online platforms (or extent of market coverage), use of agency versus wholesale distribution model, and the relative position of the platform vis-à-vis suppliers. Other considerations that might be relevant are the incremental impact of additional platform competition, and the extent of adherence to MFNs by suppliers. Whether these factors are all relevant will depend on the context of the specific market. For example, in insurance markets, it may be relatively easy for suppliers (i.e., insurance providers) not to adhere to any MFN agreement

15. It is notable that the recent decision of the UK competition authority finding an infringement of Article 101 by CompareTheMarket in home insurance is based on an effect-based approach. In its decision, the Competition and Markets Authority (CMA) notes that 'it is arguable that CTM's wide MFNs were by their very nature harmful to the proper functioning of normal competition. However, given the CMA's findings on the restrictive effects of CTM's wide MFNs, the CMA has chosen not to reach a conclusion as to whether CTM's network of wide MFNs amounted to an object infringement … '. Competition and Markets Authority, *Price Comparison Website: Use of Most Favoured Nation Clauses*, Case 50505, para. 3.5 (19 November 2020).

because of the bespoke nature of pricing depending on individual profiles, which can make it difficult to monitor. Below we discuss some of the considerations in carrying out an analysis of MFN clauses.

4.1 Relative Position of Supplier and Distributor

The size of the platform or that of the supplier has been discussed widely as a relevant factor as this also determines the market coverage of MFNs. However, the *relative* position of the platform/distributor and the suppliers is likely to be a key factor to be considered in most markets. This is because MFNs could help strengthen the position of one or a small number of larger platforms, which in turn could decrease search costs for consumers and increase competition between the suppliers.

For instance, if there are four or five large suppliers with strong brands and significant direct sales, and barriers to switching exist on the side of consumers, online platforms, such as price comparison websites, can play an important role in increasing competition between these suppliers. In this case, MFNs could benefit consumers by increasing inter-brand competition, even if there is a decrease in intra-brand competition.

Even in the case of a more fragmented supplier market, maintaining the incentives of platforms to invest in reducing search costs for consumers can be beneficial on balance to consumers if this increases inter-brand competition – for example, by promoting growth of smaller suppliers and challenging larger incumbents. In this context, and taking the example of hotel bookings, it is interesting that the Commission's support study finds that OTAs are more important for the visibility of small hotels relative to larger ones. Small accommodation providers estimate their marketing and IT costs necessary for acquiring visibility to be higher than the commissions paid to these platforms.[16]

This relative size between platforms and suppliers is not discussed as widely as other relevant factors. For instance, the report Competition Policy for the Digital Era discusses the extent of competition between platforms, stating that: 'If competition between platforms is sufficiently vigorous, it could be sufficient to forbid wide MFNs while still allowing narrow MFNs. If competition between platforms is weak, then pressure on the dominant platforms can only come from other sales channels and it would be appropriate for competition authorities to also prohibit narrow MFNs.'[17] This approach, however, offers only a partial view and significantly risks prohibiting beneficial MFN clauses, because it focuses only on intra-brand competition and not on the overall impact on consumers through intra- and inter-brand competition.

4.2 Competition Between Different Distribution Channels

Whether or not an MFN clause is likely to harm competition and consumers also depends on the competitive dynamics in the distribution layer more broadly. Specifically, distribution platforms facilitating a transaction between suppliers and consumers could also compete with the suppliers' own direct distribution channels, which by definition are not considered

16. European Commission, *Support Studies for the Evaluation of the VBER*, Final Report, p. 99 (2020).

17. European Commission, *Competition Policy for the Digital Era* (2019), https://ec.europa.eu/competition/publications/reports/kd0419345enn.pdf.

as platforms. Whether or not these other distribution channels are considered part of the relevant market will depend on the specific case. Notwithstanding the market definition, however, such competitive interaction between the direct channel and the platforms, and hence the wider constraints on a platform, should be accounted for in the overall assessment of MFNs (and selective distribution systems as well). Again, the reference to 'competition between platforms' only in the report Competition Policy for the Digital Era, and not to the potential wider constraints on a platform, represents a narrow view of potential competitive dynamics in digital markets.

The need to focus on wider constraints, and not abiding by the market definition too strictly, is even more important due to the challenges and uncertainties around defining the relevant market for online platforms. While different views regarding the precise boundaries of the relevant market can arise in any market, these are particularly stark in digital markets, and this continues to be a topic of much debate among academics and practitioners alike.[18] In this context, it is critical to have a wider focus on the competitive dynamics. By the same logic, this makes an effects-based approach more important for MFNs and for other vertical agreements involving digital environments.

18. For a discussion on market definition in multi-sided markets, *see*, e.g., L. Filistrucchi, D. Geradin, E. van Damme and P. Affeldt, *Market Definition in Two-Sided Markets: Theory and Practice*, Journal of Competition Law & Economics, Vol. 10, Issue 2, 293-339 (2014); and a response by G. Niels, *Transaction Versus Non-Transaction Platforms: A False Dichotomy in Two-Sided Market Definition*, Journal of Competition Law & Economics, Vol. 15, Issues 2-3, 327-357 (2019).

4.3 Short- and Long-Run Outcomes

In many of the cases so far (e.g., hotel bookings, insurance), one theory of harm has been the potential reduction in the incentive for platforms or distributors to compete vigorously through lower commissions. This was the case in the online hotel booking investigations where one concern was that MFNs would allow OTAs to charge higher commissions or reduce downward pressure on commissions. The same concern arises in other cases (such as the recent UK case in the home insurance market).[19] The commission rate of the concerned platform or distributor is therefore one outcome measure that needs to be analysed when assessing the effects of MFN clauses. For example, the *ex post* assessment of the hotel booking investigations in the 2017 report analysed the effect on OTA commissions before and after the ban of wide MFNs. The same was analysed by the UK competition authority in the context of an assessment of the effect of the ban on wide MFNs in the motor insurance market.

Other outcome measures that reflect consumer outcomes more directly are also (and we posit, equally) important when assessing the effects of MFN clauses, particularly in online platform markets. For instance, it is important to analyse prices of the product to consumers in the broader market and on the specific platform, as well as metrics that capture the quality of service provided by the platform to consumers. For example, MFNs can reduce search costs for consumers and improve the 'quality' of service the consumer gets from the

19. For example, the UK CMA investigated and fined price comparison platform CompareTheMarket for its wide MFNs with insurers. Competition and Markets Authority, *Price Comparison Website: Use of Most Favoured Nation Clauses*, Case 50505 (19 November 2020).

platform.[20] In this context, it is notable that not all authorities have analysed consumer outcomes when assessing MFNs. For example, while the 2017 study on wide MFNs did analyse consumer prices for hotels, the UK authority only focused on platform commissions when analysing the effect of the removal of MFNs in motor insurance, in essence assuming that higher commissions would lead to higher consumer prices.[21]

This links to the broader question around the extent to which additional competition between platforms, especially platforms which facilitate comparisons (price and non-price), improves consumer outcomes in the long run. While, in principle, higher platform competition should increase intra-brand competition, and potentially reduce commissions, there may be decreasing returns to additional competition if there are sufficient platforms in the market already. For example, it may be that an oligopolistic structure among platforms with three or four comparison websites allows for sufficient intra-brand competition, while at the same time keeping each platform popular enough to facilitate and increase inter-brand competition. Here, it is relevant to consider the potential effects of platform services on consumer trust.

---

20. Put simply, without an MFN, a supplier can offer consumers different prices in different platforms. This can increase search costs for consumers as they have to search across platforms to find the most attractive offer. While such price dispersion could be seen as beneficial as it increases intra-brand competition (i.e., competition for the same product across platforms), it is not obviously so because this either entails significant search costs for the consumer or alternatively, the consumer may not search across platforms and not identify the best offer. With an MFN in place, on the other hand, price dispersion and intra-brand competition may be lower. However, this also reduces search costs and can enhance inter-brand competition between suppliers. This effect on search costs is recognised by the 2020 support study for the Commission's evaluation of the VBER.

21. The Competition and Markets Authority, Digital comparison tools market study, Final report (2017).

Specifically, having a large number of platforms is not necessarily better for long-term consumer outcomes because any concerns regarding poor quality of service by some platforms could reduce consumer trust in all relevant platforms as a group (the large number of online flight booking platforms and lack of trust in many of them is one such example).[22] This is a key aspect to consider in striking the balance between the potential anti-and pro-competitive effects of clauses such as MFNs and in ensuring that both intra- and inter-brand competition is enhanced to the benefit of consumers.

5 HOW SHOULD JUSTIFICATIONS SUCH AS FREE RIDING BE ACCOUNTED FOR?

As discussed above, the prevention of free riding is one of the common pro-competitive benefits of MFNs and indeed of many other vertical agreements. As shown by the German experience, the scope of consumers' free riding on OTAs' investments was the key reason for the court to overturn the Bundeskartellamt (BKA) decision after the appeal by Booking.com.

In general, competition authorities, while recognising the free riding justification as relevant in principle, often do not accept the argument because of lack of concrete evidence. This is not surprising. Showing that free riding is occurring in the context of an investigation into a specific vertical agreement in a specific market context (e.g., an MFN clause or a

22. There have been concerns in the past about the reduction of consumer trust in comparison tools, for example, following proliferation of such platforms, and the European Commission led a number of initiatives to address this. *See* the discussion in European Commission, *Comparison Tools: Report from the Multi-Stakeholder Dialogue* (March 2013), https://ec.europa.eu/info/sites/info/files/consumer-summit-2013-msdct-report_en_0.pdf.

selective distribution system) is likely to be difficult because the existence of the agreement itself could be preventing such free riding. What is needed for assessing free riding is an assessment of the counterfactual world without the specific agreement.

This could be a challenge. First, the agreement in question (say, MFNs) may be used by most market players or in most countries. If this is the case, it is difficult to find a suitable counterfactual. A further challenge could be that the detrimental impact of consumers' free riding on platform businesses (or retailers using MFNs) would likely materialise only in the medium to long term and not within a few months. As noted by the Düsseldorf Court in its ruling on the BKA decision on narrow MFNs, the free riding risk will materialise only over time as consumers lose confidence in OTAs as offering the best prices, thereby switching away to the direct channel and weakening the extent to which OTAs can invigorate inter-brand competition.[23]

Nonetheless, there is a range of evidence one can bring to bear on this question. Consumer surveys are an obvious one, where consumers are asked about their online search behaviour including where they start their search, what subsequent steps they take, how many and which websites they use to search, whether they purchase from the same site as they search in and so on. Data on actual consumer search and

23. Interestingly, the BKA has recently made public an analysis of the narrow MFNs it conducted during the course of the proceedings and the results of which the Court did not accept. While the last word has not been said about this study and the BKA's case, this publication is interesting for various reasons, including its aim of empirical measurement of issues such as free riding. *See* Bundeskartellamt, *Competition and Consumer Protection in the Digital Economy: The effects of narrow price parity clauses on online sales – Investigation results from the Bundeskartellamt's Booking Proceedings* (4 February 2019), https://www.bundeskartellamt.de/SharedDocs/Publikation/EN/Schriftenreihe_Digitales_VII.html.

browsing behaviour are also available from various sources. Such data is particularly useful given it directly captures actual behaviour (and does not suffer from some of the concerns around surveys, such as being a 'stated' behaviour). Such data can help assess, for example, whether consumers typically visit the relevant distribution platform (e.g., OTA) and the suppliers' websites (e.g., hotels) on the same day. Such cross-visitations and audience overlap analysis indicate the scope of free riding in a world without the agreement (e.g., without MFN clauses or if the selection criteria for a selective distribution network is relaxed to include more online retailers).

Whatever the method, it is relevant to take account of the inherent challenges in providing concrete evidence of free riding occurring in the specific market. Arguably, what is necessary is to show the *scope or risk* of free riding rather than *actual* free riding (assuming the MFN or selective distribution in place, one is less likely to observe actual free riding).

It is also necessary to take account of such free riding analysis in the competitive assessment of the MFN under Article 101(1) and not only under Article 101(3). This can form part of the effects-based analysis through the consideration of potential outcomes in a counterfactual world without the MFN. In other words, an effects-based approach towards MFNs should involve a counterfactual analysis, which in turn should include an analysis of potential consumer search and purchasing behaviour without MFNs. One would expect that such analysis would include an assessment of whether and to what extent consumers are likely to use the platforms to search for the best offer and then undertake the purchase on the supplier's website if they find a better price in such a counterfactual (i.e., free ride). Given the various pro-competitive rationale recognised in the literature, such an approach is particularly important. This is not just for MFNs, but for vertical agreements more broadly.[24]

6 WHAT IS THE IMPLICATION FOR THE VBER?

To conclude, it is clear that the assessment of MFN clauses is an area where substantial guidance is required, particularly with the rise of digital platforms. The upcoming revision of the VBER and the Vertical Guidelines is one avenue for the Commission to provide such guidance. The economic approach discussed in this article would suggest that the current VBER remains adequate for the assessment of MFNs. The Vertical Guidelines, on the other hand, need to be updated to provide detailed guidance. The Commission's decisional practice may also assist, although it is doubtful whether there will be suitable opportunities for the Commission to open such a case under Article 101 TFEU (particularly in light of proposed regulation under Digital Markets Act which may oblige large online platforms not to use wide MFN clauses).[25] Judgments from national courts are therefore likely to be important for more clarity on this topic. Indeed, the two cases that are making their way through courts are expected to clarify the approach towards the analyses of the effects and

24. For a legal perspective on this issues, *see* P. Ibáñez Colomo, *Vertical Restraints after Generics and Budapest Bank*.

25. European Commission, *Digital Markets Act: Ensuring Fair and Open Digital Markets* (December 2020). *See* Article 5(b) of the proposal.

objective justifications of MFNs.[26] As this article discusses, from an economic perspective it is critical that MFN clauses are assessed using an effects-based analysis.

26. The two cases which are likely to be heard in the next two years include the appeal of the online hotel booking decision of the BKA involving narrow MFNs and the debate on objective justification, and the appeal of the UK CMA's decision in home insurance involving wide MFNs and the likely debate on the effects analysis.

Disruption of Online Distribution Models: What Are the Implications for the Revision of VBER and Vertical Guidelines? An Economic Perspective

Miguel de la Mano & Guillaume Duquesne[*]

1 CONTEXT

The E-commerce Sector Inquiry reveals that the growth of e-commerce has had a significant impact on companies' distribution strategies and customer behaviour.[1]

First, price transparency has increased with online trade. Consumers can instantaneously compare product and price information at almost zero (search) cost. They can switch swiftly from one distribution channel to another (online/offline). While this allows consumers to find the best

* The views expressed in this article are those of the authors.

1. European Commission, *Final Report on the E-commerce Sector Inquiry*, §§10-14 (2017), https://ec.europa.eu/competition/antitrust/sector_inquiry_final_report_en.pdf.

deal online, it has exacerbated free-riding behaviour.[2] On the one hand, consumers can use brick and mortar shops' presale services before ordering a product online. On the other hand, they can search and compare products online before purchasing in brick and mortar shops.

Second, (inter- and intra-brand) price competition has increased due to the ability of consumers to compare prices of products across several retailers. While such increased price competition has beneficial effects for consumers, it may affect competition on parameters other than prices, such as quality, brand, and innovation. While the price is a key parameter of competition between retailers, quality, service reputation, image, and innovation are essential in brand competition. Incentivising innovation or quality and keeping control over their brand's image and positioning are of major importance for most manufacturers. Also, they need to ensure the viability of their business in the mid to long term.

As a result of these market trends, manufacturers have increased their efforts to obtain a greater influence over distribution networks and better control price and quality of their products in the retail market. This has led to several changes in distribution models, such as increased direct sales by suppliers and greater use of selective distribution systems, which allow suppliers a tighter control over resale conditions.[3] Similarly, new types of vertical restrictions, such as restrictions regarding sales through online marketplaces and

2. *Ibid.*, §11: '72% of the manufacturers responding to the questionnaires explicitly acknowledge the existence of free-riding by online sales on offline services. 62% acknowledge the existence of free riding by offline retail on services (information) offered online. Approximately 40% of retailers also acknowledge the existence of free-riding behaviour both ways.'

3. European Commission, *Staff Working Document Accompanying the Document Report from the Commission to the Council and the European Parliament Final report on the*

restrictions on online advertising, as well as retail parity clauses, have become more widespread.[4]

In this context, the Commission started in October 2018 an in-depth evaluation of the Vertical Block Exemption Regulation (VBER) and accompanying Vertical Guidelines, which expire in May 2022. The results of the evaluation were published in a Staff Working Document, where the Commission notes that while the VBER and Vertical Guidelines provide a useful instrument that increases legal certainty, 'certain provisions … lack clarity, are difficult to apply or no longer adapted to the market developments that occurred since the adoption of the VBER and the Vertical Guidelines in 2010'.[5] This is notably the case when it comes to applying the existing rules to new market players that do not fit into traditional supply and distribution concepts and to new online sales restrictions.

The current rules then need to be revised to reflect this new paradigm. It gives a unique opportunity to further ground the VBER and Vertical Guidelines on sounded economic principles to avoid false positives (type 1 errors) within the digital context. Precisely, while vertical agreements may restrict competition, they may also, in many instances, allow

---

E-commerce Sector Inquiry, §§178-187 (2017), https://eur-lex.europa.eu/legal-content/EN/TXT/?uri=CELEX%3A52017SC0154.

4. *Ibid.*, §259: 'Increased recourse to vertical restrictions represent one of the most frequent reactions of manufacturers over the last 10 years to the growth of ecommerce. 56% of manufacturers that responded to the relevant question indicate that they make use of selective distribution agreements, although often limited to their high-end or new product lines.'

5. European Commission, *Staff Working Document Evaluation of the Vertical Block Exemption Regulation* (2020), https://ec.europa.eu/competition/consultations/2018_vber/staff_working_document.pdf.

firms to realise efficiencies that may not be possible absent such agreements. Over-enforcement is likely harming customers already today.

The VBER has a sound and clear economic rationale, so far as it sets a clear safe harbour for vertical restraints that are unlikely to have anticompetitive effects.[6] A safe harbour is a 'must' under the self-assessment regime that emerged from the 2004 Antitrust Modernisation regime in the EU.

Outside the VBER safe harbour, conventional economic analysis implies that a careful case-by-case assessment is required to evaluate whether the pro-competitive effects of a vertical agreement outweigh its potential anticompetitive effects. Accordingly, the Vertical Guidelines should present the possible (new) theories of harm and clearly state under which conditions these theories are likely to hold (and when it is unlikely that the adverse effects will materialise). Any presumptions should be rebuttable. It goes without saying that the rules governing different types of vertical agreements should be suitably aligned. From an economic perspective, the 'likely effect' of a vertical restraint matters more than its specific form.

In light of the above, some of the issues highlighted in the Staff Working Document are discussed below, namely a need for guidance regarding resale price maintenance (RPM), the treatment of active and passive sales restrictions and the treatment of retail parity clauses.

6. This will typically be the case when competition remains fierce even once the vertical agreement is adopted.

2 RPM: A MORE LENIENT APPROACH IS WARRANTED IN THE DIGITAL ERA

An RPM agreement is a vertical agreement wherein an upstream supplier and a downstream customer agree to the constraints on the price the downstream firm can charge end-customers. RPM can involve an upstream supplier setting the final retail price, a minimum downstream price, or a maximum downstream price. A fixed or minimum RPM is a hardcore restriction under the VBER and is therefore presumed both to be anticompetitive in all circumstances and unlikely to generate any kind of efficiency or pro-competitive effect. A hardcore restriction essentially equates RPM to a cartel infringement.

As a matter of economics, it is wrong to characterise fixed or minimum RPM as a hardcore restriction. This is both because RPM may not always have anticompetitive effects, for example, when the upstream firm has no market power and inter-brand competition is intense, and RPM can generate significant efficiencies such as reducing free-riding and incentivising investment on pre- and after-sales service.

Today, the consensus among economists, lawyers, and business practitioners is that a case-by-case approach is appropriate for assessing RPM agreements' competitive effects, even if there is debate about whether RPM should fall under the safe harbour in the VBER. The academic literature provides multiple examples of pro-competitive effects of RPM, notably reducing free-riding at the retail level,[7] ensuring that

7. Rey, Patrick, and Thibaud Vergé, *Economics of Vertical Restraints* in *Handbook of Antitrust Economics* 353-390 (Paolo Buccirossi ed., 2008). RPM in the form of minimum price can be used to avoid retailers' free-riding on the services to be provided to consumers. Imposing minimum price forces rival retailers to compete instead on the level of services – conversely, between two stores offering the same price, but different

retailers are willing to stock and promote products with unpredictable demand,[8] or promoting competition upstream by providing quality certification.[9] Accordingly, maintaining RPM as a hardcore restriction will certainly lead to inefficient vertical arrangements and under-reliance on online retailers, thereby reducing choice and harming consumers.

The few remaining practitioners that claim RPM should remain a hardcore restriction argue that other types of vertical restraints could equally solve the free-riding problem without restricting intra-brand price competition. Thus, they claim, there are less restrictive alternatives to RPM. This may be the case in some circumstances, but it is self-evident that it is not always the case.[10] Restricting price intra-brand competition

---

levels of services, consumers are likely to patronise and buy from the store offering the greater services, even if they could get the service (e.g., presale advice) in one store and still buy in the other store.

8. Deneckere, Raymond, Howard P. Marvel, and James Peck, *Demand Uncertainty and Price Maintenance: Markdowns as Destructive Competition*, The American Economic Review 87.4: 619-641 (1997). For many products, such as books or musical recordings, consumer demand is uncertain at the time the retailer orders the product from the manufacturer. If consumer demand turns out to be slack, a retailer may find itself with excess inventory and may have to offer deep discounts. Given the potential for precipitous price declines, retailers may decline to stock products, choosing instead to wait for products to prove themselves. If enough retailers take that route, untested high-quality products that could have become commercial successes may never have the opportunity to prove themselves. By setting a minimum retail price, the manufacturer may reduce price volatility, thereby encouraging retailers to take a chance on untested products or to order larger inventories than they otherwise would order. It benefits both the manufacturers of such products and consumers.

9. Marvel, Howard P., and Stephen McCafferty, *Resale Price Maintenance and Quality Certification*, The RAND Journal of Economics 15.3: 346-359 (1984). RPM can be used to solve free-riding problem when some kind of quality certification activity undertaken by a retailer is costly and can be appropriated by competitors.

10. Bennett, Matthew, et al., *Resale Price Maintenance: Explaining the Controversy, and Small Steps towards a more Nuanced Policy*, Fordham International Law Journal 33: 1278 (2009).

can prove necessary to stimulate competition on other relevant dimensions like service, quality, or innovation.

Take, for example, the case of an upstream supplier introducing new products every year. It needs to induce retailers to provide extensive (and dedicated) presales services. RPM is the most efficient and effective tool to ensure the threat of free-riding does not lead to underinvestment in such (costly) services. Otherwise, the new product will likely fail, reducing incentives to innovate in the first place and restricting inter-brand competition. Once the product is well established, it may be in the interest of the supplier (and retailers) to lift the RPM restriction and stimulate intra-brand competition to compete more effectively with other brands.

This is not to say that RPM cannot have anticompetitive effects[11] in some situations. For instance, RPM may support a collusive arrangement between suppliers (or retailers) by facilitating monitoring and enforcement.[12] But, in these cases, it is certainly more appropriate to intervene directly against the horizontal agreement. Just prohibiting RPM would not necessarily eliminate the cartel and lead to even closer information exchange agreements or explicit collusion.

Moreover, if inter-brand competition is intense, it is unlikely that a reduction of intra-brand competition will have any adverse effects on consumers. This is very relevant in the digital world. The low search costs and high transparency of online prices across different brands are likely to stimulate vigorous inter-brand competition. Thus, particularly online, the reduction in intra-brand competition due to RPM is of no

---

11. Rey, Patrick, and Thibaud Vergé, *supra* n. 7, 353:390.
12. Jullien, Bruno, and Patrick Rey, *Resale Price Maintenance and Collusion*, The RAND Journal of Economics 38.4: 983-1001 (2007).

consequence since each retailer remains constrained by competition from other brands. When RPM is observed in online markets, it is therefore relatively safe to presume it is driven by pro-competitive or efficiency motives, not a desire to keep high prices or instigate collusion.

The empirical evidence on the effects of RPM is scarce, and it gives somewhat mixed conclusions.[13] For example, as mentioned in the Staff Working Document, empirical analysis of RPM in the market for books shows that the practice may have increased consumer welfare by lowering book prices without any corresponding reduction in quantity sold.[14] Thus, without an assessment, one cannot anticipate whether pro-competitive effects will outweigh anticompetitive effects. But equally, presuming leads to over-enforcement, forcing suppliers to rely less on independent retailers, ultimately harming consumers and achieving the exact opposite outcome that antitrust enforcement intends.

In a nutshell, it is wrong and actually possibly detrimental to customers to characterise fixed or minimum RPM as a hardcore restriction. At the very least, RPM should fall under Article 5 of the VBER as an excluded restriction. In any event, at the risk of stating the obvious, firms with limited or no market power, whether suppliers or retailers, cannot rely on RPM to restrict inter-brand competition. This, in effect, implies that RPM should also fall under the 30% safe harbour. Outside this safe harbour and given the ambiguous impact of RPM when upstream supply is heavily concentrated, it is appropriate to spell out in the Vertical Guidelines the possible

13. European Commission, *Support Studies for the evaluation of the VBER*, 3.3.1.4 Econometric analysis of impact of RPM (2019), https://op.europa.eu/en/publication-detail/-/publication/93f52e95-a92e-11ea-bb7a-01aa75ed71a1.

14. European Commission, *Staff Working Document Evaluation of the Vertical Block Exemption Regulation*, *supra* n. 5, p. 173.

economic justifications and the theories of competitive harm associated with RPM.

3 ACTIVE AND PASSIVE SALES RESTRICTIONS: AN ARTIFICIAL DELINEATION

Exclusive distribution enables a manufacturer to reserve for itself or to designate only one retailer in a particular territory and to protect that retailer against other (exclusive) retailers actively approaching customers in the exclusively allocated territory ('active sales') or responding to unsolicited requests from individual customers ('passive sales'). The VBER treats restrictions on active and passive sales differently: restrictions on passive sales are hardcore restrictions, whereas restrictions on active sales are not.

The economic literature does not support such a difference in the treatment of these restrictions. Regardless of selective distribution, both types of restrictions can have anti- and pro-competitive effects. Precisely, the literature has identified anticompetitive effects of sales restrictions, such as dampening inter-brand competition,[15] or restoring market power[16] as well as pro-competitive ones, such as the

15. Rey, Patrick, and Joseph E. Stiglitz, *Vertical Restraints and Producers' Competition*, No. w2601, National Bureau of Economic Research (1988). Rey, Patrick, and Joseph E. Stiglitz, *The Role of Exclusive Territories in Producers' Competition*, Rand Journal 26.3 (1995).

16. Hart, Oliver, et al., *Vertical Integration and Market Foreclosure*, Brookings Papers on Economic Activity, Microeconomics: 205-286 (1990). O'Brien, Daniel P., and Greg Shaffer, *Vertical Control with Bilateral Contracts*, The RAND Journal of Economics 23.3: 299-308 (1992). RPM can be used as a commitment device to protect upstream rents. A manufacturer maximises its profit by selling the right to distribute to only one retailer. However, *ex post* it has an incentive to break this agreement and sell to additional retailers. The overall effect is that, absent a commitment device, the manufacturer is unable to extract the full rent associated with its market power,

protection against free-riding on retailers' services,[17] or the efficient use of retailer's information.[18]

None of these papers point to a distinction between active and passive sales. Furthermore, for both active and passive sales restrictions, while the pro-competitive effects can materialise regardless of the manufacturer's market power, the anticompetitive effects are likely to be significant only when they involve manufacturers with substantial market power and/or networks of parallel restraints covering a substantial part of the market.

Accordingly, as a matter of economics, active and passive sales restrictions should be treated in the same way and not treated as hardcore restrictions. Rather than resorting to a formal and, to a large extent, arbitrary approach aiming to classify active and passive sales, it may be worth using a more effects-based approach. The treatment of firms that use sales restrictions would depend of the market share they hold and the possible efficiency justifications associated with such restrictions.

To the contrary, the current (artificial) distinction between passive and active sales certainly leads already to over-enforcement and harm to consumers, as done with RPM. This is, for example, the case when preventing 'geographic' price discrimination it could in many instances enable supply to customer groups with low ability or willingness to pay.[19]

because it cannot commit itself to not cutting prices on later contracts. In this context, sales restrictions can act as a commitment devise.

17. Mathewson, G. Frank, and Ralph A. Winter, *An Economic Theory of Vertical Restraints*, The RAND Journal of Economics 15.1: 27-38 (1984).

18. Rey, Patrick, and Jean Tirole, *The Logic of Vertical Restraints*, The American Economic Review 76.5: 921-939 (1986).

19. To understand how 'geographic' price discrimination can improve welfare, focus on the case of a manufacturer distributing a product for two groups of customers A and

Ergo, the current rules, by retaining hardcore restraints, may hurt precisely those customers that may be the most income constrained and create a wider wedge in the Single Market.

4 PRICE PARITY CLAUSES, NO GROUND FOR BLOCK EXEMPTIONS OR BANS

Price parity clauses or Most Favoured Nation clauses (hereafter 'MFN clauses') are used in business models characterised by agency relationships between suppliers and online platforms. Under such (often long-term) contractual agreement, the supplier commits to charge on the platform a price that is not higher than the price charged on other platforms.

In the online world application of MFN clauses, a distinction has emerged between so-called wide and narrow MFN clauses. Wide MFN clauses specify that better terms cannot be offered to any party, or via any channel, than those offered to the contracting party. For example, a hotel owner might be required by an Online Travel Agency ('OTA') to always advertise on the OTA's website the best available prices. Narrow MFN clauses state instead that better terms cannot be offered via the supplier's online direct channel. A hotel owner that contracts with a certain OTA would thus offer lower prices on the websites of other OTAs and on offline channels. However, the price offered on the OTA's website would have

B, with unit demand for each product. Consider customers A have a high valuation for the product, equal to EUR 100, while customers B have a low valuation, equal to EUR 10, still above the marginal cost of producing the product. If the manufacturer is not allowed to price discriminate through, e.g., selective distribution, then it sets prices at EUR 100 to maximise profit. At these prices, customers with low valuation do not consume. By price discriminating, through selective distribution, the manufacturer can set different prices for both categories of customers. By setting the price at EUR 100 for high-value customers and EUR 10 for low-value customers, the manufacturer serves both customers, thereby expanding output.

to be at least as favourable as the one displayed on the hotel's own website.

While RPM as a practice is considered a hardcore restriction of competition, the legal and economic analysis of retail MFN clauses' implications and status is still ongoing.

Some countries in Europe have banned both narrow and wide MFN clauses (e.g., France, Italy, Austria, and Belgium).[20] In other countries, courts or competition authorities have decided to ban only wide MFN clauses (e.g., Germany, Sweden, and the UK) on a case-by-case basis. The latter policy is in line with the recommendation that stems from economic analysis, as of today.

In this respect, the economic literature on MFN clause is still evolving, and many open questions are yet to be addressed. In turn, empirical evidence remain scarce. But the limited evidence available supports the conclusion (as with other vertical restraints) that MFN clauses have the potential for both pro- and anticompetitive effects.[21]

More precisely, MFN clauses have efficiency-enhancing effects that are beneficial for consumers. They can remove the risk of free-riding including showrooming and webrooming, e.g., that consumers use a platform to compare products, enjoy additional services (such as customer reviews), and then purchase their favoured product directly from the producer or on a cheaper platform. As a result, they can ensure

20. France adopted the 'Loi Macron' in August 2015. Austria, Italy, and Belgium followed in banning all types of parity clauses with laws entering into force in 2017. Colangelo, Margherita, *Competition Law and Most Favoured Nation Clauses in Online Markets* in *New Developments in Competition Law and Economics*, Springer, Cham, 295-317 (Klaus Mathis & Avishalom Tor eds., 2019).

21. European Commission, *Support Studies for the evaluation of the VBER, supra* n. 14.

that platforms are not discouraged from investing in their platform's quality.[22]

Furthermore, MFN clauses reduce search costs for consumers, thereby promoting inter-brand competition.[23] Precisely, the platform improves information flows by collating and aggregating quantitative and qualitative data about suppliers, price, and product characteristics. Such data is often provided in multiple languages, supporting access to suppliers worldwide. Also, modern markets are often characterised by differentiated products and services. A platform makes it easier for users to compare offerings and identify the best bargain. In the case of OTAs, this function has significant effects on small- and medium-sized hotels. Such small or boutique hotels would otherwise find it too costly and risky to engage in direct advertising and absorb the high cost of pay-per-click advertising. In sum, the reduction in search costs and the availability of better information reduce sellers' market power and profit margins to the benefit of consumers.

MFN clauses may also lead to competition concerns through three fundamental mechanisms.

First, platform (wide) MFN clauses may limit competition between platforms on the level of the commissions they charge to suppliers. This leads to higher commissions and eventually to higher prices being charged to final consumers.[24] The logic is as follows. Assume the online platform

22. Wang, Chengsi, and Julian Wright, *Search Platforms: Showrooming and Price Parity Clauses*, The RAND Journal of Economics 51.1: 32-58 (2020).

23. This type of argument can be traced back to an earlier literature on the impact of search costs on market equilibria. Salop, Steven, and Joseph Stiglitz, *Bargains and Ripoffs: A Model of Monopolistically Competitive Price Dispersion*, The Review of Economic Studies 44.3: 493-510 (1977).

24. Fletcher, Amelia, and Morten Hviid, *Retail Price MFNs: Are They RPM 'at Its Worst'*, ESRC Centre for Competition Policy Working Paper: 14-5 (2014).

charges a fee for each transaction, and a wide MFN clause is in place. In such a scenario, the platform may be incentivised to increase its fees (or not reduce them). This is because a wide MFN clause protects the platform from the risk that a supplier will react to an increase in the commission it has to pay by increasing the product price on that platform only.

Second, platform (wide) MFN clauses may also hinder entry into the retail market because they effectively lock all prices at the same level.[25] Precisely, absent MFN clauses, if incumbent platforms decide to charge high commissions, potential competitors will have the incentive to enter or expand into the market by offering a lower commission rate that would attract favourable treatment from suppliers. With retail MFN clauses, suppliers would be unable to offer a better price through these cheaper platforms, which invalidate the business model of entry or expansion based on lower commission rates. By the same token, they can also discourage suppliers from making investments that result in lower prices. This is because the lower price would have to be charged on the platforms, thereby limiting the supplier's ability to steal sales.

Third, MFN clauses can facilitate collusion by increasing price transparency and stability.[26] After all, under an agency model, the imposition of (wide) MFN clauses by leading platforms would result in identical pricing and terms.

25. Boik, Andre, and Kenneth S. Corts, *The Effects of Platform Most-Favored-Nation Clauses on Competition and Entry*, The Journal of Law and Economics 59.1: 105-134 (2016). Johnson, Justin P., *The Agency Model and MFN Clauses*, The Review of Economic Studies 84.3: 1151-1185 (2017).

26. Ezrachi, Ariel, *The Competitive Effects of Parity Clauses on Online Commerce*, European Competition Journal 11.2-3: 488-519 (2015).

While real and potentially serious, when the supplier or the platform is dominant, these concerns are likely to be of limited relevance when there is enough competition between platforms and suppliers. Even if intra-brand price competition is softened, there is still competition on all other dimensions that matter for consumers. Furthermore, when competition between platforms is vibrant, the supplier can terminate the relationship with a platform that seeks excessive commissions.[27]

As a matter of economics, the welfare effects of MFN clauses are a priori ambiguous, such that they are ultimately best evaluated on a case-by-case basis. The effect of MFN clause will certainly depend on the exact setting that is being examined, i.e., whether the obligations are narrow or wide, whether competition is more intense at the supplier level or at the platform level (and whether suppliers can remove their products from platforms), whether platforms facilitate consumers' search for prices and product characteristics, thereby benefiting customers.

In particular, a less permissive approach to wide MFN clauses appears reasonable; all else equal a platform with a wide MFN clause has greater incentives to raise its commission than if there is only a narrow MFN clause. Similarly, a

27. Johansen, Bjørn Olav, and Thibaud Vergé, *Platform Price Parity Clauses with Direct Sales*, University of Bergen (2017). Johansen and Vergé (2017) also show that parity obligations can benefit consumers. They argue that the Boik and Corts (2016) and Johnson (2017) result that wide parity obligations lead to higher fees and therefore higher retail prices may not hold when suppliers can remove their products from high fee platforms. Then, parity obligations can lead to higher or lower fees, depending on the degree of competition between the suppliers. In particular, parity obligations are unlikely to harm consumers and may actually benefit them when suppliers are sufficiently close substitutes, and the suppliers compete fiercely. In their setting, narrow and wide parity obligations are equivalent in terms of their outcomes.

new entrant platform may be prevented from gaining a foothold in the market when the offer of lower commission fees to suppliers does not result in lower retail prices for consumers. This would not hold in the presence of narrow MFN clauses by incumbent platforms. However, that is not to say that a blanket policy against even wide MFN clauses is justified. Since both narrow and wide MFN clauses may potentially have both anti- and pro-competitive effects, ultimately, economics suggest that any such presumptions based on wide or narrow parity clauses should be rebuttable.

In light of the above, the VBER and Vertical Guidelines should explicitly include the consideration of MFN clauses. They could do so in a way likely to provide more clarity on the potential competition concerns, potential efficiencies, and best-practice approach to analysing their economic effects. Importantly, if the supplier and the platform markets are both fragmented, MFN clauses are likely benign and most likely pro-competitive. Thus, if neither the upstream supplier nor the distribution platform has a market share above 30% there should be no concern. In other words, the VBER already adequately balances the benefits and competition risks of parity clauses. To the contrary, MFN clauses by dominant platforms are not and should not be block exempted. There is no per se legality in concentrated markets under EU competition law.

5 TIME TO MOVE TOWARDS A MORE SYSTEMATIC EFFECTS-BASED APPROACH

The efficiency justifications that have been discussed in the economic literature equally apply to both online and offline businesses. This is also true for the anticompetitive motives underlying the adoption of vertical restraints. However, a new balance has to be found. It requires on one side to allow suppliers and retailers to adopt the exclusivity constraints within the digital environment and, on the other side, to preserve the liberty of consumers to shop wherever they want.

Without an in-depth assessment, one cannot a priori anticipate whether pro-competitive effects will outweigh anticompetitive effects. But equally, presuming leads to over-enforcement, forcing suppliers to rely less on independent retailers, ultimately harming consumers and achieving the exact opposite outcome that antitrust enforcement intends. It implies that the mere concept of hardcore restriction may become irrelevant in the digital area. At the very least, vertical restraints should fall under Article 5 of the VBER, as an excluded restriction.

To conclude, it is still to be considered whether some practices also merit to fall under the safe harbour. While a safe harbour is a 'must' under the self-assessment regime, great care is required. Since network effects are prevalent and tipping is difficult to reverse online, one could forego the safe harbour for online vertical restraints to avoid false negatives (type 2 errors) within the digital context.

The Future of Vertical Restraints: The View of a National Enforcer

Jacques Steenbergen[*]

From our perspective, vertical restraints organising territorial restrictions or price maintenance have always been a major source of concern.

1 WHERE WE COME FROM

It may be useful to recall that when the Regulation 330/2010[1] and the 2010 Guidelines[2] were discussed, we insisted with other National Competition Authorities (NCAs) on maintaining the list of hardcore restrictions in the block exemption and considered it imperative to see, in particular, Retail Price

* This contribution is partly based on J. Steenbergen, 'Challenges to Enforcers', in C.S. Catalin, A. Looijestijn-Clearie. M. Veenbrink and S. Tans (eds.), *New Directions in Competition Law Enforcement*, Radbout Economic Law Series, 1-17 (Wolf Legal Publishers, Nijmegen 2020).

1. Commission Regulation (EU) No 330/2010 of 20 April 2010 on the application of Article 101(3) of the Treaty on the Functioning of the European Union to categories of vertical agreements and concerted practices, OJ L 102, 23.4.2010, pp. 1–7.

2. Commission Notice, *Guidelines on Vertical Restraints*, OJ C 130, 19.5.2010, p. 1.

Maintenance (RPM) clauses as restrictions by object. Economists wished to extend the scope of the new economic approach and the effects-based assessment to all vertical restrictions, and, in particular, to RPM clauses. Tired of endless discussions, the NCAs obtained Article 4(a) on RPMs but did not block the insertion of the reference to a rebuttable presumption in §47 of the Guidelines. In the opinion of the Belgian Competition Authority (BCA), the presumption with respect to RPM clauses would be almost impossible to rebut. But I have to accept that §47 of the Guidelines has created a gap between the expectations of a significant number of stakeholders and the intentions of the authorities.

2 WHERE WE ARE

Many competition authorities now also see some non-digital verticals as a priority. Not because we like verticals to be a problem or because we would be able to deal with them in our comfort zone, but because market studies, such as studies comparing prices in supermarkets in neighbouring countries,[3]

3. *See*, e.g., for Belgium: Belgische Mededingingsautoriteit, *Prijsniveau in supermarkten* (2012), https://www.bma-abc.be/sites/default/files/content/download/files/20120213-studie_prijsniveau_supermarkten.pdf, which is being updated at the request of the Minister for the Economy in light of Instituut voor de nationale rekeningen, Prijzenobservatorium, Jaarverslag 2017, hoofdstuk III, *Vergelijking van het consumptieprijsniveau in België, Duitsland, Frankrijk en Nederland* (2018). *See also* Federaal Planbureau, *Consumptieprijzen in België en de buurlanden – Aandachtspunten voor het beleid*, Working Paper 13-12 (October 2012). *See*, for Luxembourg, Rapports de l'Observatoire de la formation des prix, *Analyse du niveau et de l'évolution des prix des produits de grande consommation au Luxembourg et dans la Grande Région* (2018), https://gouvernement.lu/fr/support/recherche.gouv_odc%2Bfr%2Bpublications%2Brapport-etude-analyse%2Brapports-observatoire-formation-prix%2Brapport-thematique-ofp%2Brapport-thematique-ofp-0071.html. *See*, for the Benelux, Secretariaat-Generaal van de Benelux Unie, *Territoriale leveringsbeperkingen in de detailhandel in België, Nederland en Luxemburg* (2018), http://www.benelux.int/files/4115/2696/8143/beneluxstudie.pdf. *See*, for the Euro zone, European Central Bank

showed significant price differences that could not be explained by objective cost factors. They are, in particular, concerned about the impact of a wide variety of territorial supply constraints (TSCs).[4] These concerns have, among others, prompted an initiative by the Benelux Secretariat General.[5]

Certainly, for smaller authorities, it is important that the most harmful vertical restrictions are qualified as hardcore restrictions. When restrictions such as RPM clauses would need to be assessed as restrictions by effect that may benefit from the De Minimis Notice,[6] we might as well give up our advocacy efforts towards Small and Medium Size Enterprise (SMEs), as most can claim that their agreements taken separately are well below the thresholds and have only a marginal impact on markets. But when SMEs do not even feel concerned by the most basic rules of competition, it is unlikely that there will ever be a competition culture in socioeconomic environments where the overwhelming majority of undertakings are SMEs.

Several NCAs have asked the Commission to take up vertical cases in order to give guidance by enforcement. This has resulted in welcome decisions on fairly straightforward

(ECB), *Grocery prices in the Euro area: Findings from the Analysis of the Disaggregated Price Dataset*, Issue I (2015), https://www.ecb.europa.eu/pub/pdf/other/art01_eb201501.en.pdf.

4. *See*, e.g., Secretariaat-Generaal van de Benelux Unie, supra n. 3.

5. *See*, e.g., Benelux Unie, *Benelux Ambtelijke Top Economische Zaken bespreekt toekomst Retailmarkt* (2017), https://www.benelux.int/nl/nieuws/benelux-ambtelijke-top-economische-zaken-bespreekt-toekomst-retailmarkt.

6. Communication from the Commission – Notice on agreements of minor importance which do not appreciably restrict competition under Article 101(1) of the Treaty on the Functioning of the European Union (De Minimis Notice), OJ C 291, 30.8.2014, pp. 1-4.

RPM restrictions (even though on online markets) and on geo-blocking.[7]

I do not see this development as a reversal of the search for a more economic approach. On the contrary, it is the result of confrontation with economic reality. That also applies to the arguments that we must be able to deal with some infringements as hardcore by object. Some types of behaviour can be identified *ex ante*, while others only on a case-by-case assessment of their impact.

3 VERTICALS AND THE DIGITAL ECONOMY: THE CASE OF E-COMMERCE

In the first place, e-commerce makes it easier to buy cross-border. But geographic restrictions, such as geo-blocking, also have an increased impact, as was clearly shown by the European Commission's sector enquiry.[8] The way competition authorities deal with e-commerce illustrates that we can meet the challenge with existing concepts, provided that we carefully look at the facts and interpret the rules and concepts in light of evolving markets:

- E-commerce transactions are assimilated with passive sales under §52 of the 2010 Guidelines.[9] It follows that a refusal to deal will usually be a hardcore restriction by object.
- Hardcore restriction rules, such as the prohibition of RPM clauses, apply to online as they do to offline businesses, i.e., as

7. Commission Decisions in AT.40469 *Denon & Marantz*, C(2018) 4774 final, 24.7.2018; AT.40465 *ASUS*, C(2018) 4773 final, 24.7.2018; AT.40181 *Philips*, C(2018) 4797 final, 24.7.208; AT.40182 *Pioneer*, C(2018) 4790 final, 24.7.208; and AT.40436 *Ancillary Sports Merchandise*, C(2019) 2172 final, 25.3.2019.

8. European Commission, Final Report on the e-commerce sector inquiry, COM(2017) 229 final, 10.5.2017.

9. *Guidelines on Vertical Restraint*, supra n. 2.

restrictions by object – *see* the four recent Commission Decisions on RPM on online markets.[10] In these Decisions, the Commission focused on the supplier, and that may well signal a tendency, and geo-blocking in e-commerce was sanctioned in the Commission's Decision of 25 March 2019 in *Nike*.[11]

4 THE REVIEW OF THE VBER

In the above-mentioned context, the contribution of the BCA to the public consultation on the review of the Vertical Block Exemption Regulation (VBER) and the Guidelines can be summarised as follows:

- The BCA emphasises the positive impact of the VBER and the Guidelines but considers that they need to be expanded in order to give more guidance,[12] especially (but not only) in view of the development of the digital economy.
- In view of the *Coty* case law,[13] we would like to see more guidance on the concept of 'luxury products', e.g., in respect of the indications of reduced prices in the context of selective distribution contracts.
- We would like to see more guidance with respect to platforms, e.g., on the criteria to distinguish between platforms that can be qualified as distributors or as intermediaries; and also on the definition of geographic markets for online platforms, the calculation of market shares (e.g., in respect of zero-price markets) and the possible need to review the 30% market share threshold.

10. Commission Decisions in AT.40469 *Denon & Marantz*, C(2018) 4774 final, 24.7.2018; AT.40465 *ASUS*, C(2018) 4773 final, 24.7.2018; AT.40181 *Philips*, C(2018) 4797 final, 24.7.208; AT.40182 *Pioneer*, C(2018) 4790 final, 24.7.208.
11. Commission Decision in AT.40436 *Ancillary Sports Merchandise*, C(2019) 2172 final, 25.3.2019.
12. 'Guidance' can be given with the preferred legal certainty in the VBER-2 or in the Guidelines.
13. Judgment of the Court (First Chamber) of 6 December 2017, *Coty Germany GmbH v. Parfümerie Akzente GmbH*, C-230/16, §32.

- We consider that the VBER or Guidelines should address the concern about the exchange of sensitive information between suppliers and distributors in case the supplier is also a direct competitor in the retail market.
- We strongly insist on the need to keep RPM as a hardcore restriction.
- We would like to see a more precise qualification of other infringements that exclude the benefit of the VBER.

www.ingramcontent.com/pod-product-compliance
Ingram Content Group UK Ltd.
Pitfield, Milton Keynes, MK11 3LW, UK
UKHW020843290926
15470UKWH00004B/1526

9 789403 53243